MW01139858

Applying AutoSketch®
A Step-by-Step Approach
for AutoSketch® 3.0

Wayne J. Elinger
Assistant Dean
Spokane Community College
Spokane, Washington

John J. Horstketter
CAD/CIM Instructor
Spokane Community College
Spokane, Washington

GLENCOE

Macmillan/McGraw-Hill

Lake Forest, Illinois
Columbus, Ohio
Mission Hills, California
Peoria, Illinois

Copyright © 1993, 1990 by the Glencoe Division of Macmillan/McGraw-Hill School Publishing Company.

All rights reserved. Printed in the United States of America. Except as permitted under the United States Copyright Act, no part of this publication may be reproduced or distributed in any form or by any means, or stored in a database or retrieval system, without prior written permission from the Publisher.

Send all inquiries to:
GLENCOE DIVISION
Macmillan/McGraw-Hill
3008 W. Willow Knolls Drive
Peoria, Illinois 61614

ISBN 0-02-668091-2 (Work-Text)
ISBN 0-02-668092-0 (Instructor's Guide)

1 2 3 4 5 6 7 8 9 10 96 95 94 93 92

TRADEMARKS
AutoSketch, AutoCAD, and DXF are registered trademarks of Autodesk, Inc.

Any representation of the AutoSketch name and logo throughout this book and related promotion is not to be construed as an endorsement on the part of Autodesk, Inc.

Dedication

To our wives and children for their support
in the development of this book.

Acknowledgments

John and Wayne would like to thank the staff at Glencoe for their work and dedication to this book. A special thanks goes to Debra Baxter, Technical Education Editor, and Trudy Muller, Director of Technical Education.

The authors also wish to thank Spokane Community College, Terry Wohlers, and the staff at Autodesk, Inc.

Glencoe/McGraw-Hill thanks David E. East, Industrial Technology Instructor, for his contributions to the manuscript.

Table of Contents

931102

Introduction

Applying AutoSketch guides you though a new way of drawing. The step-by-step techniques you learn while using AutoSketch® will change the way you draw in the future. The new methods explained in this text will let you draw faster and change your mind more often without worrying about erasures or the amount of time it would take to retrace something. The ease with which you can change your drawing when you change your mind is one of the most impressive features of AutoSketch.

Computer-Aided Drafting

AutoSketch is software used for computer-aided drafting (CAD). To take advantage of this method of drawing, you must learn to think differently about the drawing process. You must plan your every move to take advantage of CAD possibilities. You must also be willing to change your mind as you draw. When you use a computer, you won't lose a lot of time when you copy or revise a drawing. With AutoSketch you are now free to express yourself with the power of CAD techniques.

AutoCAD®

Learning about AutoSketch is also your first step in becoming acquainted with AutoCAD. The AutoCAD program is the industry standard for microbased CAD programs (programs designed for small-scale, or personal, computers). It can be used to produce any type of drawing – from a highly technical engineering drawing to a fine art drawing. AutoCAD software is so popular that it is now changing the way we think about and use drafting. In AutoSketch software you will find many of the techniques and commands used in AutoCAD.

Word Processing

You can also create drawings in AutoSketch and import them into a document that you are creating with a word processing or desktop publishing program. For example, an activity near the end of this book guides you through the process of copying an AutoSketch drawing into a WordPerfect® file.

What's New in This Edition

This edition of *Applying AutoSketch* includes the new commands and features for the AutoSketch Version 3 software. Some existing commands have also been enhanced. Here are some of the highlights:

- Ellipse command. New command for creating an ellipse.
- Pattern Fill. Formerly the Fill Region command. Provides new patterns for filled objects.
- Polyline. Formerly the Polygon command. Functions have been expanded.
- Quick Text. Similar to the former Text command on the Draw menu.
- Text Editor. Provides a dialogue box for adding and changing text. Text may be imported from an outside source.

- Part Clip. Stores segments from a drawing.
- New Attach modes have been added.
- New choices for arrowheads for dimension lines have been added.
- Scroll bars. Used for panning the drawing or scrolling through directories.
- Icons. Drawings, patterns, and fonts can now be selected by icon or by name.

A new feature for this edition is the activity described above for importing AutoSketch drawings into a WordPerfect file.

Stories about AutoSketch users are also new. People of all ages use AutoSketch, including the second grade students you can read about at the end of Unit 6.

About the Text

We assume that you have very limited or no experience in the use of AutoSketch. Therefore, the text takes you though skill-building exercises and problems. It gives you step-by-step directions for making, changing, and saving drawings.

We also assume that you rely on this text to teach you about AutoSketch. Watch what happens on the computer screen as you do the exercises and problems. Don't be afraid to write notes in the book or highlight important parts. By doing so, you'll make the book even more useful for yourself. Ad you work through the text, the activities help you develop more ability and confidence in using CAD.

UNIT 1

What Is CAD?

Objective:

■ *To understand how the development of the microcomputer has influenced the methods of making drawings.*

From Sticks and Rocks to Microcomputers

Throughout history, drawings have been used to communicate ideas, but the tools and materials to make them have changed greatly. The cave dweller who used sticks to paint on rocks would be amazed to see how drawings are produced today. We now have the tools to produce drawings with precise details and measurements. The types of material on which drawings are made have changed considerably—from stone to canvas, from paper to plastic film.

The greatest advancement in creating drawings has taken place in the last 30 years with the introduction of the computer. The computer has the power and capability to do the work of many people. It can calculate mathematical formulas, help write and correct letters, draw graphs and diagrams, and do drafting problems.

The first computer was a large floor-model machine that worked in only certain air temperature and humidity levels. Now a computer is a relatively small machine (some can even be held on your lap) and operates well under almost any condition. Today's *microcomputer* (small-scale computer) has all the capability of its 30-year-old cousin, with greater power and speed to do drawing-related tasks.

Computers in Industry and Art

Drawing for industry with a computer shortens the process and makes a drafter more productive. *Computer-aided drafting* speeds up the older methods used in drawing. Companies using CAD can do more work in less time and increase their profits.

The microcomputer has not only transformed the industrial world but has also recently made a tremendous impact on the artistic world. Computers are now used in producing art, movies, and *animation*. In animation, a series of drawings is projected rapidly, one after the other, so that the image seems to move. Computer artists use software such as Animator™ to create graphic images that before were only a dream. By blending pictures on film with computer-animated images, they can make lifelike motion pictures. These new images can take you into outer space or under the surface of the ocean without leaving your seat.

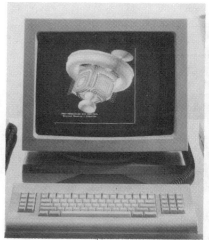
Courtesy of Sun Microsystems, Inc.

Courtesy of Autodesk, Inc.

You and CAD Software Work Together

All this power is at your fingertips, and you are limited only by your imagination. But this new tool, the microcomputer, can only be as productive and creative as the person using it. Putting together all the power, speed, and capabilities of the microcomputer still requires an operator—you—and CAD software. AutoSketch provides the tools necessary to produce drawings with greater ease, accuracy, and creativity. Once you master AutoSketch, you are on your way to entering the 21st century.

 *Key Terms*

microcomputer   computer-aided drafting   animation

Let's Review

 *Questions*

1. What is one of the major differences between making drawings 30 years ago and drawing today?

   _____

   _____

2. What makes today's computer different from the first computer used by industry?

   _____

   _____

   _____

   _____

3. List three reasons why the microcomputer is a better drawing device than traditional ones like pencils and measuring tools.

   _____

   _____

   _____

4. Name some of the ways computers are used at your school that change the way you do your assignments.

   _____

   _____

   _____

Extend Your Knowledge

1.   Look in computer magazines or visit a computer store to learn about the different things software packages can do. Find the names of separate software packages that will

   ■   create text
   ■   do mathematical operations
   ■   create computer graphics.

2.   If possible, collect CAD drawings from relatives or friends who work with CAD programs. Some of the fields that use CAD programs include Architecture, Interior Design, and Civil Engineering. Can you think of others? Discuss with your class the drawings you have collected.
   Submitted by David East, Bloomington, Illinois

3.   Find information about three different microcomputers and explain what makes them different.

4.   Go to the library and find information on the history of how computers were developed. Write a report on your findings.

5.   Write a report that compares computer animation to other types of animation. Try to include examples of movies that use the types of animation described in your report.

6.   Get into small groups (of about three people). You may also try to do this alone. Predict what is going to happen in the near future. Use the year 2000 as a point for which you predict what the computer will be like. What will it look like? What will it be able to do? How much memory will it hold as a single unit? How will it be connected to other computers?

How to Use
Applying AutoSketch

Objective:
■ *To understand how this text and its units are organized.*

What to Expect in Each Unit

In this text you will be using an easy-to-follow format. Each unit may include

■ objectives

■ explanations of the commands being introduced

■ exercises to build your skills

■ helpful hints

■ cross-references to the *AutoSketch Reference Manual, Installation and Performance Guide,* and *Tutorial*

■ key terms to learn

■ questions

■ problems to test your skills

■ activities to extend your knowledge of CAD.

Unit objectives begin each unit. They identify unit concepts and help you understand how you will apply them. Explanations and illustrations of the new concepts are provided next in the unit.

Beginning with Unit 4, each unit goes through exercises or step-by-step instruction to help you increase your understanding and skills. Complete the exercises or steps as you read the text so that you build your skill level as you go through the unit. As you do them, you should produce the same results shown in the drawings in the text.

As you read, you will find hints that suggest shortcuts, alternate methods, and ways to avoid common errors. You are encouraged to bend page corners, paper clip pages, or highlight information that you find especially useful. Then you can quickly refer to it as you do the exercises.

Located in the right-hand margins are cross-references to the AutoSketch manuals. They list the page numbers in the *AutoSketch Reference Manual*, the *Installation and Performance Guide*, or the *Tutorial*. You can read more in these guides about features explained in the text. This margin area will also be useful for your own notes.

Key Terms are listed at the end of units. These lists will help you identify and learn the terms introduced in the unit. Learning the new terms in each unit helps you build your knowledge as you move from one unit to the next. The first time a term is used, it is in *italics*.

Questions are asked at the end of each unit to help you check your understanding of new ideas and measure your progress.

Problems are included at the end of units to test your skills. Extend Your Knowledge activities help you develop an understanding of CAD before or after you use the computer.

Optional Problems and Appendixes

Additional, Optional Problems can be found in the back of the text. The Optional Problems are meant to challenge the AutoSketch user, and you are encouraged to try them. Besides these extra problems, you can try to make drawings and artwork that have not been done before with AutoSketch. When you have created an especially fine drawing, please feel free to send it to Autodesk, Inc. (the company that designed AutoSketch) or to the authors:

Wayne Elinger
John Horstketter
Spokane Community College
N. 1810 Greene St.
Spokane, WA 99207

Autodesk, Inc.
Drawing Archives
2320 Marinship Way
Sausalito, CA 94965

We will try to include your drawings in new editions of *Applying AutoSketch*.

After the Optional Problems are the Appendixes. They give you details on operating AutoSketch and provide other reference material.

How to Use the Text

We have several recommendations for using this text:

- First, skim the text to get an idea of the material it covers and how it is organized.

- Read through each unit and complete the questions at the end before you start drawing on the computer.

- Check your basic understanding of the key terms; then as you begin working on the computer, follow the directions closely.

- The *commands* (tasks to be done by the computer) are listed in this text in the order that should be followed to achieve the results shown. If you are having trouble with a particular command, the first thing to do is to try the command sequence again. Then instead of giving up, try it again. If that still doesn't work, reread the material in the text, and do the command sequence one more time. You could also use the cross-reference to find information about the command in the AutoSketch manuals. As you become more familiar with the commands, using AutoSketch will become easier and less frustrating.

■ To learn AutoSketch most effectively, follow the order of the material in the text. Don't jump around. This text has been organized so that what you learn in one unit is used in the next unit.

■ Use the blank pages and areas in the text to take notes or write comments to refer to later.

Key Terms

cross-references   commands

Giving Kids a Learning Boost

Almost everybody knows that AutoSketch can help you learn to draw. Now teachers are finding that it helps young kids learn in other ways. One obvious example is story telling. Children first write a story and then are inspired to illustrate it, or the other way around. In either case, both language as well as drawing skills are practiced and improved.

One art teacher uses AutoSketch to introduce fourth graders to the basics of architecture. Students learn one-point perspective and design an entire house. They use AutoSketch to create floor plans and to show the house from different perspectives. The children become especially excited by the fact that the drawings they do with AutoSketch are so much better than those done with pencil and paper.

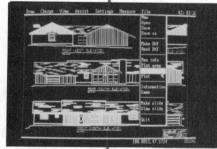

Courtesy of Autodesk, Inc.

AutoSketch has also promoted group learning. Some students draw better than others. Some are better at math or science or language arts. When they work with AutoSketch in groups, each child has a chance to shine. Most kids enjoy AutoSketch so much that they often volunteer to stay after school; they shine a lot.

Let's Review

Questions

1. What area in the text provides space for your notes and comments as well as cross-references to the *AutoSketch Reference Manual, Installation and Performance Guide,* and *Tutorial?*

   _____

   _____

2. Where will you find the additional problems to do in this text?

   _____

   _____

3. What should you do if a command doesn't work as described in *Applying AutoSketch?*

   _____

   _____

   _____

   _____

Extend Your Knowledge

1. Look carefully through the guides provided by Autodesk, Inc. and become familiar with the format. Look up a few of the cross-references to the guide listed in *Applying AutoSketch.*

2. Set up a folder to hold notes, short-cuts, sketches, and drawings as you work through the text. Keep the folder in a handy location so you can refer to it and add new terms. Later, you may want to use AutoSketch to design a cover for your folder.

UNIT 3

Learning about the AutoSketch Workstation

Objective:

■ *To identify the various parts of the typical AutoSketch workstation.*

A workstation is made up of a computer and monitor, *input devices*, and *output devices*. Input devices are equipment used to send information and instructions to the computer. Output devices receive information and images from the computer. Input

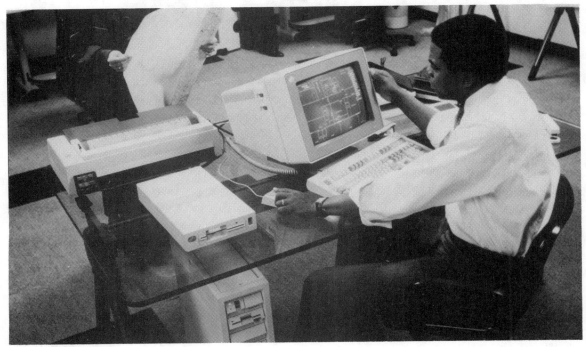

Courtesy of IBM Corporation

and output devices are attached to the computer. The AutoSketch program was written to work with certain types of computers, input and output devices, and connections between them. You can find details about this hardware (equipment) in the *AutoSketch Installation and Performance Guide*.

The Computer and Monitor

AutoSketch is a *PC-CAD* program. That is, it is CAD software written for use with a personal computer (PC). Like all the other types of computers, a PC has an electronic "brain" called the central processing unit (*CPU*). The CPU carries out the instructions of the program and has enough memory to store data and instructions for a short time. The computer has other sections of memory to store information for longer periods of time. The CPU also sends information to and receives information from other parts of the computer.

*AutoSketch®
Installation
and
Performance
Guide*
pp. 3-5
39-79

pp. 43-49

Courtesy of Radio Shack, a Tandy Corporation

The monitor displays the data being passed back and forth on a screen of a CRT (cathode ray tube). AutoSketch, like other graphics software, requires a screen of reasonably high resolution. This means that it must produce clear, sharp images in which you can see fine details.

Courtesy of Autodesk, Inc.

Courtesy of Texas Instruments

Input Devices

The *keyboard* attached to the computer is one input device. It is used to type or enter information and instructions, mainly in the form of letters and numbers.

pp. 39-42

Besides the keyboard, you can use several other kinds of equipment to draw with AutoSketch. One kind is a *mouse*, a drawing tool that you hold in your hand. When you roll it on the tabletop or other surface, these movements are translated into locations on the screen. It also has buttons that input data to the computer.

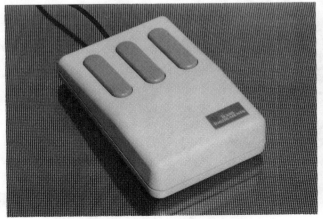

Courtesy of Texas Instruments

Another type of input uses a puck and digitizer. The puck looks like a mouse and usually has 3 to 16 buttons. The puck is different from a mouse because, instead of a tabletop, you move the puck over a digitizer. The digitizer is shaped like a pad. It translates the movement to the screen as you move the puck over it.

You might also use a joystick or a touch pad. You have probably used joysticks with handles and buttons to play computer games. A touch pad gets its name from the way it works—you touch your finger on a pad to control movement on the screen.

Output Devices

Output devices produce hard copy (a paper copy of what is displayed on a monitor screen) for drawings. You can use a laser or graphics (dot matrix) *printer,* or a pen *plotter.* Laser and dot matrix printers show images as series of dots. A laser printer provides the best quality of printing. A plotter uses pen and paper to create an inked drawing.

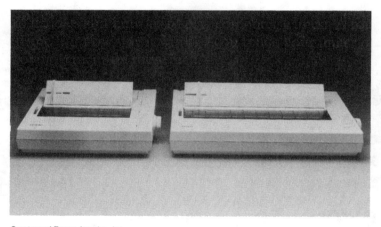

Courtesy of Epson America, Inc.

Courtesy of Houston Instrument

AutoSketch®
Installation
and
Performance
Guide

pp. 51-79

Key Terms

output devices   input devices

CPU   PC-CAD

mouse   keyboard

plotter   printer

The Decision

by Kelly Hasset

"Hey Matthews!" came a voice from somewhere from the depths of the hallway, "I'll meet you by your locker," the voice said.

Brian Matthews raced to his locker with anticipation. When he finally weaved his way through the excited crowd to his locker, he gasped in astonishment. There, waiting casually by the locker, was Mark Collins, star of the football team. Everyone looked up to the handsome, popular senior. Why was he here, wishing to converse with a lowly junior?

Mark, smiled effortlessly, "Hey, there's this party going on at my house tonight. Wanna come?" Brian, too stunned to say anything, just nodded.

"Great!" exclaimed Mark. "See you there!" and with that, Mark disappeared into the bustling crowd of students.

Everyone was having a fantastic time when Brian arrived at the party. Mark, who was chatting with a few teammates, sauntered over to him. "Brian, come with me, I've got a craving." He grabbed Brian by the wrist and dragged him from the magnificent elaborence of the living room to the darkness of the kitchen. Mark flicked on the light and grunted, "Want some?"

Brian stared blankly at him, "Some of what?"

"Some of this," and as Mark spoke, he removed a tiny capsule filled to the brim with cocaine out of his pocket. Brian's chin almost dropped to the floor.

"Cocaine?" Brain gasped.

"Sure, why not? It's good for you. Gives you energy. Especially for the big game tomorrow night." As Mark spoke, the capsule slipped from his fingers. As it fell to the floor, the cocaine spilled all over the clean floor. "Oh no!" Mark yelled. He fell to his knees, breathing heavily. His arms shot out blindly as he searched for the fatal drug.

As Brian watched him, he got a sharp pain in his stomach. The sight of Mark searching was like watching a sick dog look ravenously for a dry bone. Mark, the hero, calm, handsome popular Mark. With an angry cry, Brian bolted out the door and disappeared into the night.

As Brian ran, he kept saying to himself, "You did the right thing. Drugs can really mess up your life." But he didn't reassure himself very much. All he had to look forward to was the football game. But Brian didn't even get that small pleasure.

At 4:45 the next morning, star of the football team and drug addict Mark Collins died of a drug overdose.

Kelly wrote this story when she was in the sixth grade at Sauquoit Valley Elementary School in Sauquoit, New York. She drew the illustration with AutoSketch. Her story won regional and New York state anti-drug essay contests. Since then, Kelly has continued to use AutoSketch in school. For example, in the eighth grade she used AutoSketch to create drawings in Technology and Social Studies classes.

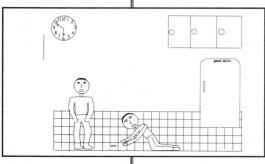

Courtesy of Autodesk, Inc.

Let's Review

Questions

1. List the parts of a typical AutoSketch workstation.

   _____

   _____

   _____

2. What are input devices? List three examples.

   _____

   _____

3. What are output devices? List two examples.

   _____

   _____

Extend Your Knowledge

1. Find a computer magazine in the library. Photocopy pictures of different types of computers, monitors, keyboards, input devices, and output devices. Make a poster that shows examples of these types of equipment. Compare the examples you found with those found by your classmates.

2. Visit a computer store and ask for a demonstration of a computer and its input and output devices.

3. Compare the following monitors:

   ■ monochrome
   ■ color graphics
   ■ high resolution graphics.

   Explain the differences that you notice. You may want to visit an engineering office, a local college, or a computer store to see how they differ.

4. Find information about input devices for CAD operations. Decide which input device you think is best and explain why. Find the cost of the device you have chosen.

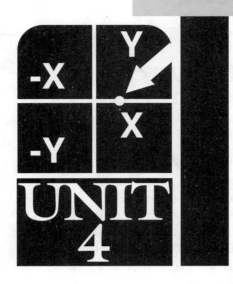

Understanding Coordinate Systems

Objectives:
- To understand coordinate systems and how each system works.
- To use three forms of coordinate systems to enter information in computer-aided drawing.

To learn to draw lines accurately with the computer, you will need to understand coordinate systems. First, what is a coordinate system? To answer this question, look at the two crossed lines below. The left-to-right (horizontal) line is called the *X-axis*. The up-and-down (vertical) line is called the *Y-axis*. At the crossing (*intersection*) of these two lines is the beginning point for all measurements. This intersection is called the origin point. In the coordinate system, this point is given the value of 0.

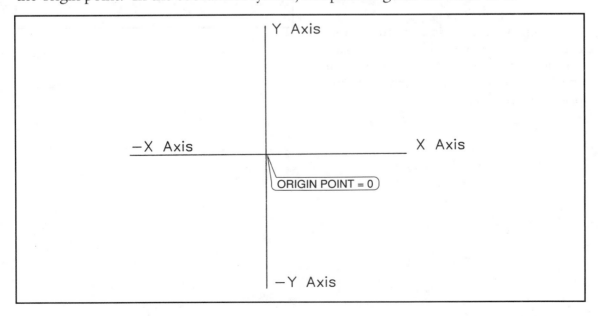

The Absolute Coordinate System

How can you use the X- and Y-axes to locate other points? On the graph to the right there are equally-spaced short lines crossing the X-axis and Y-axis. These lines divide the axis lines into units that can be used to measure horizontal and vertical distances from the origin point. The values that correspond to these units are called coordinates. You can locate any point by giving its coordinate values. The horizontal value is always given first in a set of coordinates.

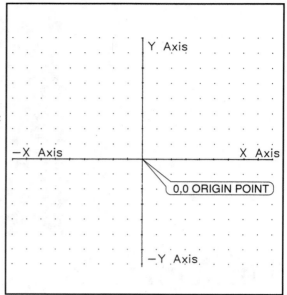

To locate a point by using coordinates on the graph, follow these steps:

1. Begin at the origin point.
2. Measure 5 units to the right along the X-axis.
3. Draw a vertical line up from this point.
4. Go back to the origin point.
5. Measure 4 units up along the Y-axis.
6. Draw a horizontal line to the right from this point until it crosses the vertical line drawn in step 3.

The point where these two lines cross has the coordinates 5,4. This means that it is 5 units to the right of the origin point on the X-axis and 4 units up from the origin point on the Y-axis.

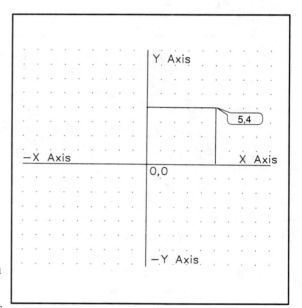

What are the coordinates of points to the left of the origin point? To show the X coordinate for a point on the left side of the origin point, use a negative sign in front of the X-axis value. To locate a point below the origin point, place a negative sign in front of the Y-axis value. On the graph below, notice three sets of coordinates that use negative signs for locations of points to the left of the Y-axis or below the X-axis.

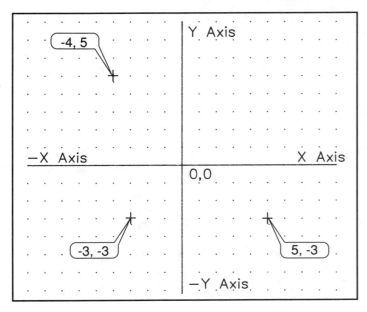

You have just learned to use one form of the coordinate system. This first coordinate system is usually called *absolute coordinate*. In this system, each point is compared to the 0,0 intersection of the X- and Y- axes.

Exercise 1

Locate and label each point on the graph below by finding its X,Y coordinates. The first point is already marked on the graph.

Starting point:
    2,1

Point 1: 7,1

Point 2: 7,3

Point 3: 5,3

Point 4: 5,5

Point 5: 2,5

Point 6: 2,1

Connect these points with lines. What type of figure have you drawn?

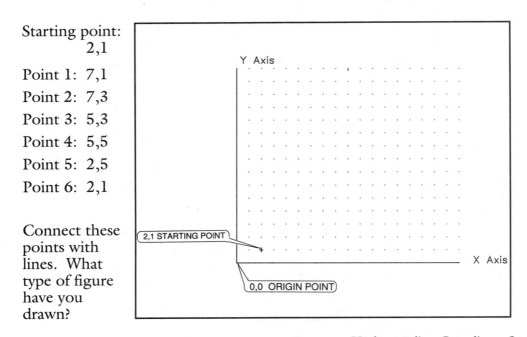

✔✔✔✔✔ *Exercise 2*

For the coordinate locations in the drawing, list X and Y values for each point in the provided spaces.

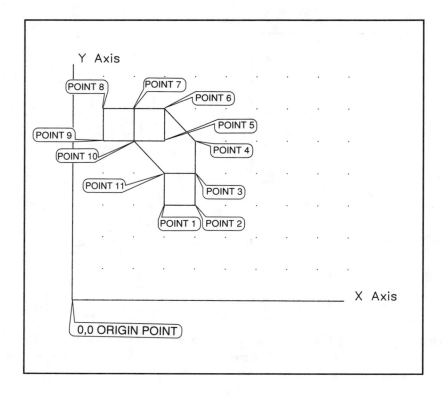

Point 1:_____

Point 2:_____

Point 3:_____

Point 4 _____

Point 5:_____

Point 6:_____

Point 7:_____

Point 8:_____

Point 9:_____

Point 10: _____

Point 11: _____

The Relative Coordinate System

A second type of coordinate system is called the *relative coordinate* system. It is similar to the absolute coordinate system since locations of points are based on X-axis and Y-axis values. In this system, however, each new point is found by comparing its location to the position of the previous point, not to 0,0.

You can see an example of locating points using the relative coordinate system on the graph on the next page. The coordinates of the new point are relative (compared) in location to the starting point, 2,0. That point becomes the origin point referred to in giving relative coordinates for the starting point. The new point is 6 units to the right. Vertically, the position of the new point doesn't change from the previous point. Therefore, the relative coordinates of the new point are 6,0.

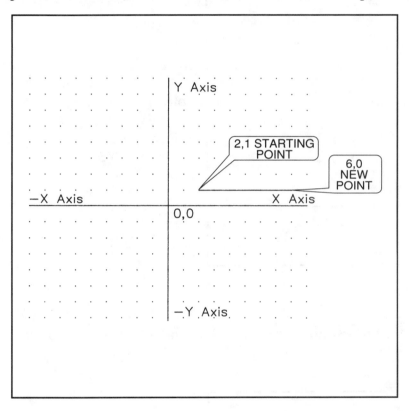

✔✔✔ *Exercise 3*

Locate the points on the graph below. Mark the relative point locations. After you have entered all the points on the graph, connect the points in order and see what figure you have drawn. The "R" stands for relative.

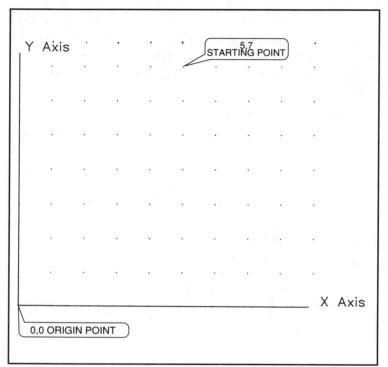

Starting point: 5,7

Point 1:   R(-2,-5)
Point 2:   R(5,3)
Point 3:   R(-6,0)
Point 4:   R(5,-3)
Point 5:   R(-2,5)

✔✔✔ *Exercise 4*

Indicate what the coordinates should be for each of the points marked on the graph.

Starting point: 3,2

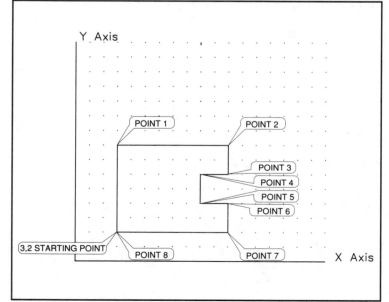

Point 1: R _____

Point 2: R _____

Point 3: R _____

Point 4: R _____

Point 5: R _____

Point 6: R _____

Point 7: R _____

Point 8: R _____

The Polar Coordinate System

The last of the coordinate systems is the *polar coordinate* system. With this system, you indicate the length of the line from the starting point to the point you want to locate (or the distance you wish to move away from your starting point). You then provide an angle or direction at which you want the line to move away from the horizontal.

On the graph to the right, what is the size of the angle formed by the line drawn and the horizontal? Yes, it is 35°. When you give polar coordinates for a point, the first value is the length of the line drawn from the starting point. The second value is the number of degrees in the angle. An example of polar coordinates is 4,35.

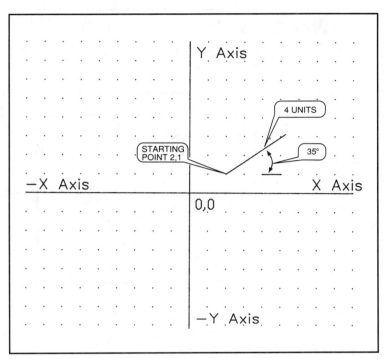

✔✔✔ *Exercise 5*

Enter the polar coordinates of the shape below in the spaces provided. Move around the shape clockwise as you list coordinates. The "P" stands for polar.

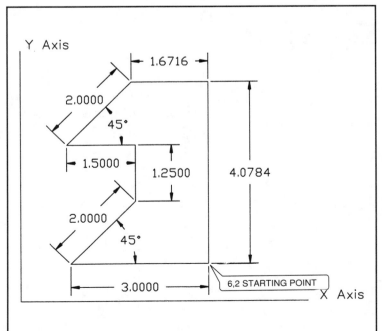

Starting point: 6,2

Point 1:   P _____

Point 2:   P _____

Point 3:   P _____

Point 4:   P _____

Point 5:   P _____

Point 6:   P _____

Point 7:   P _____

With AutoSketch you can indicate coordinates of points in three ways. How you enter coordinates depends on which coordinate system—absolute, relative, or polar—you want to use to locate the point.

▶ *Hint:*

Use the drawing shown here to help you figure out angles greater than 90°.

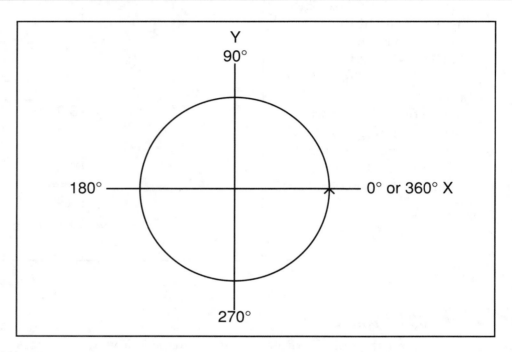

Key Terms

X-axis	absolute coordinate
Y-axis	relative coordinate
intersection	polar coordinate

Let's Review

 *Questions*

1.   How do you locate points using the absolute coordinate system?

_____

_____

_____

2.   How do you locate points using the relative coordinate system?

_____

_____

_____

3.   How do you locate points using the polar coordinate system?

_____

_____

_____

4.   In the absolute coordinate system, which of these sets of coordinates locates a point to the left of the Y-axis and below the X-axis?

A. -X,Y   C. -X,-Y

B. X,-Y   D. X,Y

5. Where is the 0,0 coordinate located?

_____

_____

Problems

For each of the following drawings, list the coordinates of the points. Try to use all three coordinate systems—absolute, relative, and polar—to locate the points. Move around the shape clockwise as you list coordinates.

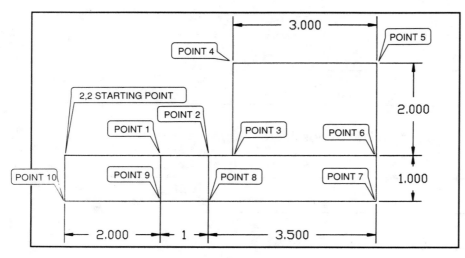

1. Starting point: 2,2

Point 1: _____   Point 6: _____

Point 2: _____   Point 7: _____

Point 3: _____   Point 8: _____

Point 4: _____   Point 9: _____

Point 5: _____   Point 10: _____

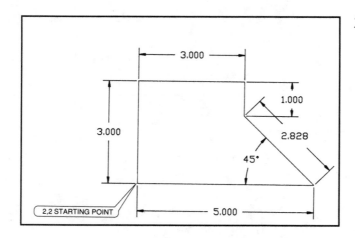

2. Starting point: 2,2

Point 1: _____

Point 2: _____

Point 3: _____

Point 4: _____

Point 5: _____

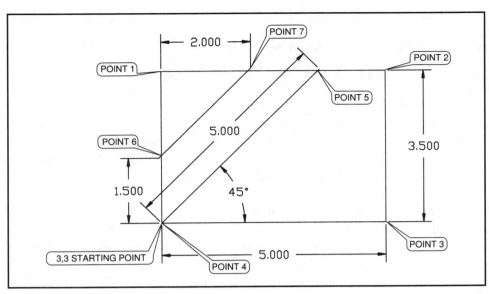

3. Use relative coordinates to find Point 4 and polar coordinates to find Point 5.

Starting point: 3,3

Point 1: _____

Point 2: _____

Point 3: _____

Point 4: _____

Point 5: _____

Point 6: _____

Point 7: _____

Extend Your Knowledge

1. Develop a drawing of a familiar object. Give the coordinate values of the drawing to someone else and have them duplicate the drawing by using the coordinate values.

2. Find out what the term "cartesian coordinates" means. Try looking in a dictionary or an encyclopedia. Report back to the class.

3. Find out how machinists use the absolute coordinate system in their work. If possible, visit a machine shop or a machine shop class at a trade school in your community.

pp. 43-44

Teaching Future Inventors with AutoSketch and Lego/Logo

Lockhart Middle School might not sound like a school for inventors. But that's where Chip Bashinski is hard at work training the next generation of Henry Fords and Robert Fultons. Bashinski is a technology teacher at the Orlando, Florida school. He uses AutoSketch along with a product called Lego/Logo to teach young inventors about science and engineering.

You are learning to use AutoSketch, but what exactly is Lego/Logo? Well, Lego is the company that makes those little, plastic building bricks with the same name. The company also makes a line of products called Lego/Logo. Each Lego/Logo product includes various types of Lego bricks and connectors, up to three motors, a battery pack, a computer interface box, and the software called Logo.

In their Exploring Technology class, Bashinski's seventh-graders use the Lego Technic II Motorized Transmission set. After they become familiar with the set's components, Bashinski gives them what he calls a challenge activity. This involves designing and constructing a motorized model. One activity requires the students to design and build a working model of a magnetic levitation train. This type of train can travel at speeds up to 212 miles per hour.

Working in groups of three, students first sketch their designs on paper. Then they refine them on the computer with AutoSketch. "What's great about AutoSketch," says Bashinski, "is that they can change things, move things, mirror much easier than they could on paper, where they would have to erase things and redraw."

After completing a design, each group sets out to build its model. This, according to Bashinski, is the most challenging part of the activity because they must be able to drive the trains. In the case of a monorail train, that means figuring out how to drive wheels that are in a horizontal position. This type of wheel moves along a central rail as opposed to typical vertical wheels. Activities like this help kids learn to think and solve problems.

When the members of a group finish building their train, they connect it to the computer with the interface box. Next they write programs, called procedures, that actually make the train run. Writing programs for computerized motor control may sound like more than a challenge for seventh-graders, but Logo's simple commands make it easy, says Bashinski. Typing 100 on the computer, for example, makes the train run for 10 seconds. Typing RD makes it reverse direction.

Throughout the project, student's document everything they do in what are called inventor's notebooks. The notebooks contain AutoSketch drawings and notes on all their design, construction, and programming activities for the project. So if their model doesn't work when they run their Logo program, they can refer to their drawings and notes and back track to the point at which a mistake was made. In less than three months, they learn advanced scientific and engineering concepts taught in many two-year colleges.

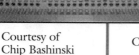

Courtesy of
Chip Bashinski

Courtesy of AutoDesk, Inc.

Getting Started with AutoSketch

Objectives:

- To locate the sections of an AutoSketch screen.
- To use the arrow pointer to select objects and menu items.
- To learn how to enter coordinates on the keyboard to select points.
- To use the hand pointer to select objects for editing.
- To understand the use of dialogue boxes.

Moving Around the AutoSketch Screen

Before you can start drawing, you need to become familiar with the AutoSketch display screen and how to indicate locations on it. When you enter AutoSketch, you will see on the screen a graphics display similar to the one on the next page.

p. 5

At the top of the screen is the menu bar. The names listed are the menu sections of AutoSketch. A *menu* is a list of commands the computer will perform and features that you can use. At the right side of the menu bar is a number with a percent sign next to it. This is a memory meter. The number indicates the amount of computer memory consumed by the drawing you are working on. This number will change as more items are placed on the drawing screen. When you begin a drawing, the value is 1%. As you add lines, circles, text, and other items to the drawing, the value will increase until it reaches 100%. At this point AutoSketch will indicate that no more elements can be stored for that drawing.

pp. 5 - 6

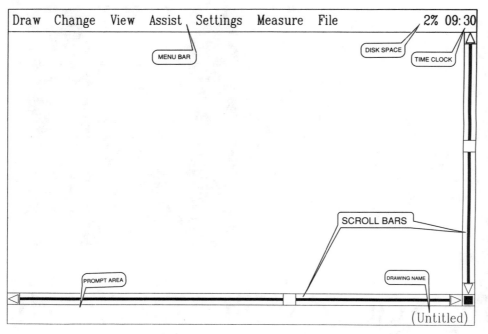

Draw   Change   View   Assist   Settings   Measure   File   2% 09:30

MENU BAR

DISK SPACE

TIME CLOCK

SCROLL BARS

PROMPT AREA

DRAWING NAME

(Untitled)

At the far right side of the menu bar is the time clock. When you begin drawing with AutoSketch, the clock tells you the time according to the 24-hour system. Drawing with AutoSketch is so fascinating that you may forget how much time is passing while you draw. The time clock will help you remember.

At the bottom left of the screen is the prompt area. With a prompt, AutoSketch tells you what command is currently in use and reminds you about information you need to enter. At the far right the name of the drawing on which you are working is displayed. When you begin a new drawing, "(Untitled)" is displayed in this space. After you assign a name to a drawing, that name is displayed every time you look at the drawing.

p. 6

Between the menu bar and the prompt line area is the drawing area. This is the part of the screen (enclosed in a box) where you can place the drawing elements.

Across the bottom of the screen is a long wide line with an arrow at each end. The same type of line appears on the right side of the screen. These lines are *scroll bars* that are used to help you get the drawing back to the center of the screen. The right scroll bar moves the drawing up and down. The bar across the bottom moves the drawing left and right.

Let's try moving around the screen.

1.   Load AutoSketch.

▶ *Note:*

To install AutoSketch, refer to the Installation and Performance Guide provided with the software. (The method you use to load AutoSketch depends upon your computer system. One way is to type SKETCH at the DOS prompt for the directory where the software is stored.)

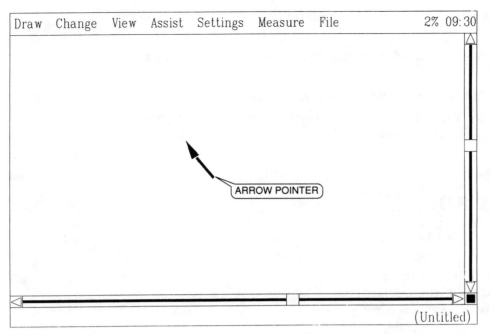

When you enter AutoSketch, you will see the *arrow pointer* on the screen. This arrow pointer is used to select menus and commands.

2. Move the arrow pointer around the screen.

You can move the arrow pointer by pressing an arrow key on the keyboard, moving a mouse, moving a puck over a digitizer pad, or moving your finger around a touch pad.

Using the Keyboard

If the keyboard is your only input device, you will need to use the following steps to practice moving the arrow pointer.

1. Press one of the **Arrow** keys.

2. Press the **Page Up** (PgUp) key.

3. Move the arrow again.

Do you notice the difference in distance the arrow moved? If you use the keyboard's arrow keys without the Page Up key, the pointer will move a short distance.

4. Press the **Page Up** key again, and then try the **Arrow** key.

Movement should increase even more. But do you notice that you have less control in locating the arrow pointer?

5. Press the **Page Down** (PgDn) key, and move the arrow.

Pressing this key should reduce the movement of the arrow pointer and improve control so that you can indicate points more accurately.

p. 6

p. 7

pg. 35

As you use this book, there are other keys on the keyboard that you can use. They are

- the Insert key–use to select objects, menus, menu items, and points
- the Home key–use to move the arrow to the menu bar
- the End key–use to move the arrow back to the point it was at when you used the Home key.

Selecting Menus and Menu Items

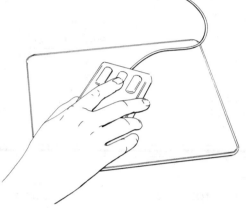

To "select" or "pick" means to choose information to send to AutoSketch. If your input device is a mouse, you select by pressing the *pick button*, usually the first one on the left.

If you are using some other pointing device (like a joystick or a digitizer puck), you will also use a button to select or pick.

In this text, whenever we use the words "select" or "pick," we mean that you should press the button on a pointing device if you are using one, or strike the Insert key if the keyboard is your only input device. Let's try picking a menu and menu items.

1. Move your arrow pointer to the menu bar, and move it first to the left and then to the right.

Do you see an *outlining block* or highlight appear around any of the names in the bar?

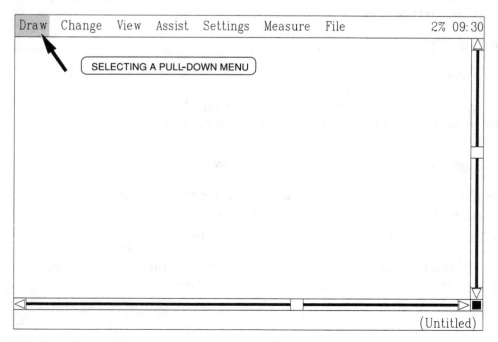

AutoSketch®
Tutorial

pp. 7-8

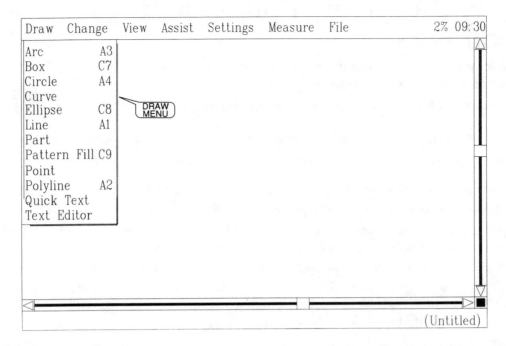

When a highlighted area is produced around a word, AutoSketch is telling you that this name can be selected to bring down a menu of commands called a *pulldown* menu.

2.   Move the pointer until the **Draw** menu name is highlighted and pick it.

The Draw menu should appear under the menu name.

3.   Now move the pointer down until one of the commands on the **Draw** menu is highlighted and pick it.

After you make a selection, it becomes an active operating command to AutoSketch. The pulldown menu disappears, and a prompt related to the command you selected appears at the bottom of the screen.

4.   To cancel this command, press the **F1** key on your keyboard.

F1 is a function key for the Undo command, and you will learn more about it in Unit 6.

▶ *Hint:*

> Later on when you draw, you should cancel a command by selecting another menu item. If you use the Undo command, AutoSketch will also erase the last element you drew.

5.   Now select a different menu to view another list of commands.

6.   To close a menu without selecting another menu or a command, point to an empty area of the screen, and pick it. Or press the **Ctrl** (Control) key and the C key at the same time.

The screen should look the way it did when you first entered AutoSketch. Notice that only one menu can be displayed at a time.

Using the Arrow Pointer and Scroll Bars

AutoSketch®
Tutorial

p. 6
pp.12-13

Besides picking menus and menu items, the arrow pointer is also used to indicate positions when you draw.

1.   Select the **Draw** menu and the **Line** command.

The prompt "Line Enter point:" will appear at the bottom of the screen.

2.   Move the pointer to any location in the drawing area and pick it.

This point is the starting point of your line. The prompt "Line To point:" asks you to select an ending point for the line.

As you use the Line command, you will see a line appear on the screen connecting the last point you selected and the location of your arrow pointer. This *rubber band* line shows you where a line would be drawn if you pick the point marked by the arrow pointer. When you select the endpoint of the line, AutoSketch adds the line to your drawing. You will see the rubber band line while you are using several AutoSketch commands.

3.   Pick another point to finish the line.

The line will appear on the screen. The prompt "Line Enter point:" returns because AutoSketch assumes that you want to continue drawing lines.

4.   Draw several lines. Place some on both sides of the screen.

Now try moving the drawing with the scroll bars.

5.   Select one of the open squares on either scroll bar. Move the square in the direction of the part of the drawing you want to view.

Before you can continue, you need some space on the screen.

6.   To clear the screen, select the **File** menu and the **New** command. Autosketch displays a dialogue box asking what you want to do with your drawing. You will learn about dialogue boxes later in this Unit 7.

7.   Pick **Discard** since you don't need to save your drawing yet.

Using Coordinates to Draw with AutoSketch

pp. 31 - 34

In the drawing you have done so far, you used a pointing device (like a mouse or the arrow keys) to select starting and ending points for lines. You can also use the coordinate systems you learned about in Unit 4 to give locations for items you want to draw.

When you use coordinates to select points, you can tell AutoSketch the exact distance you want between them and at what direction lines should be drawn. You give AutoSketch these measurements in *drawing units*. These units can stand for inches, centimeters, feet, meters, or any other unit of measurement that you need for a drawing.

When AutoSketch prompts you to enter a point, type coordinates on the keyboard instead of picking them with a pointer.

The Absolute Coordinate System

Let's enter coordinates to draw some lines.

1.   Select the **Line** command.

2.   To select the first point for a line, type **2,1**.

Check that it is correct by looking at the prompt area on the screen. If you make a mistake, use the Backspace key to remove the wrong characters.

3.   Press **Enter**.

▶ *Hint:*

On your keyboard, this key might not be named "Enter." For example, it could be labeled with an arrow or called the Return, Send, Next, or New Line key. In this text, we use Enter to indicate when you should press this key to send information to the computer.

4.   For the second point, type **7,1** and press **Enter**.

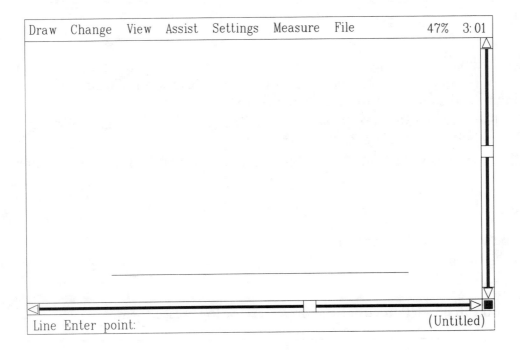

To draw this line, you used the absolute coordinate system. The units measured the distance from the origin point 0,0. In AutoSketch, 0,0 is located at the lower left corner of the drawing area.

The Relative and Polar Coordinate Systems

1. Type **2,1** and press **Enter** to start the next line.

2. Type R(**6,2**) and press **Enter**.

▶ *Hint:*

You can enter R in either the uppercase or lowercase form.

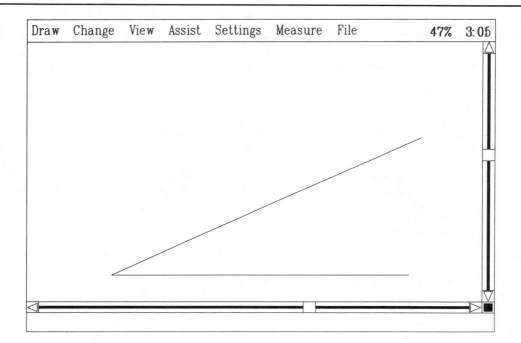

In this coordinate entry, you used the relative system. The second point is 6 units to the right of the first point and 2 units up from it. The R tells AutoSketch to figure the location of the second point from the first point you entered, not 0,0.

If you had used the absolute system to enter the second point, what would the coordinates be? (If you said 8,3, you are right!)

3. Clear the screen. You can use the **New** command from the **File** menu, or press **F1** twice.

4. Select the **Line** command, type **3,2** and press **Enter**.

5. Type **P(2.5,120)** and press **Enter**.

▶ *Hint:*

You can enter P in either the uppercase or lowercase form.

The P stands for the polar coordinate system. The 2.5 tells AutoSketch to draw a line from the first point 2.5 units long. The 120 means that AutoSketch will draw the line at a 120° angle from the first point. The angle tells AutoSketch in what direction to draw the line.

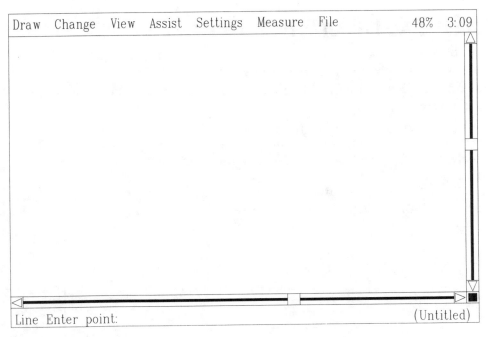

6. Clear the screen.

   Let's try using all three systems (absolute, relative, and polar) to enter coordinates for the same drawing.

7. Select the **Polyline** command from the **Draw** menu.

8. Enter absolute coordinates **2,2** for the starting point.

9. Then enter polar coordinates **P(4,0)** to draw the first line.

10. Now use the relative coordinate system by entering **R(-2,3).**

11. To complete a triangle, enter **2,2**.

Your drawing should look like the one below.

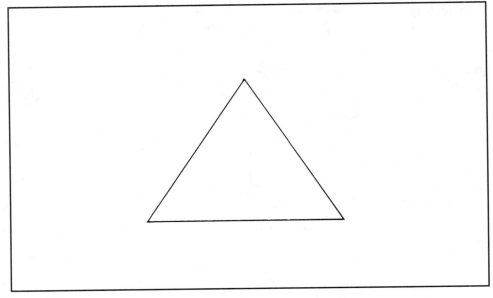

12. Clear the screen.

Selecting Objects for Editing

AutoSketch®
Tutorial
pp. 18 - 20

After you have done some drawing, you may want to change what you have drawn. This changing is referred to as "editing." The commands on the Change menu (like Erase, Move, and Stretch) can be used to edit a drawing.

1. Draw three lines anywhere on the screen.

2. Select the **Change** menu and the **Erase** command.

What happens to the arrow pointer? It changes to a *hand pointer*. Your drawing area will look similar to the one below.

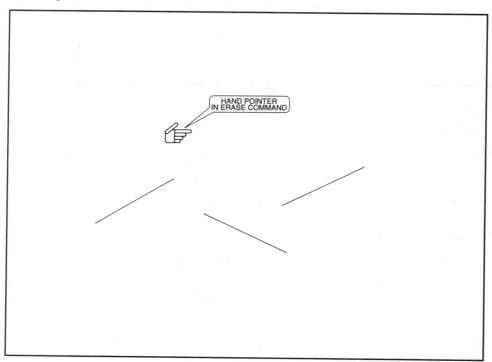

Instead of selecting an item for drawing, the hand pointer selects drawing elements for editing. The hand changes back to an arrow when you select a Draw command.

3. Move the hand pointer until the fingers touch one of the lines you have drawn, and select it.

The line you selected will disappear.

Crosses/Window Box

With the hand pointer, you can select individual elements of a drawing—like a line, a circle, or a box. But what if you want to change several elements? To edit several elements at a time, you can use the *crosses/window box* feature. It will reduce the amount of time it will take you to change your drawing.

1. Move the hand pointer to an empty area to the right of a line. Don't touch any of the other lines. Pick this location.

The prompt at the bottom of the screen should read "Erase Crosses/window corner." The point you selected will become the first corner of a rectangular box, or "window."

2. Move the pointer to the left so that the box touches one of the lines on the screen.

A box made of dotted lines will appear. This is a crosses box. Any element within the box or crossed by one of its lines can be changed.

3. Select the second corner of the box.

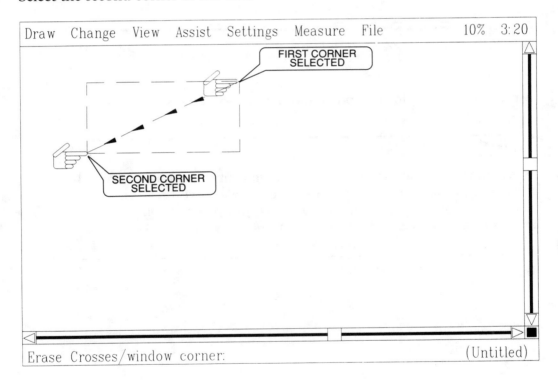

Any line contained in or crossing the crosses box should disappear.

4. Pick a point in an empty area of the screen below and to the left of a line for the first corner of another box.

5. This time move the pointer to the right.

The lines of the box that appears should be solid. This is a window box. Only elements completely contained within the box will be changed.

6. Move the pointer until the entire line is within the box.

7.　Select the second corner of the box.

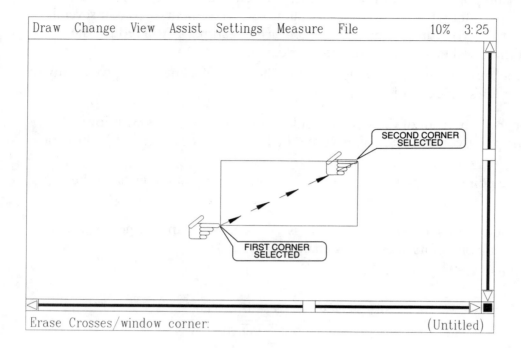

Only the lines that begin and end within the box should disappear.

► *Hint:*

As you draw and edit, you will often change your mind about what command to use. You might also make a mistake as you select a point or an object to change. To start over, just pick the command again, or pick a new command and continue working.

Dialogue Boxes

AutoSketch lets you change settings and modes (ways the computer displays elements and carries out commands) by using a *dialogue box*. A dialogue box appears when you select commands from the Settings or File menus. It temporarily covers part of a drawing on the screen.

For some dialogue boxes, you can change several settings and modes in one step.

Let's look at a dialogue box like that.

1. Select the **Settings** menu and the **Attach** command.

The dialogue box below should appear in the middle of your screen.

Draw	Change	View	Assist	Settings	Measure	File		1%	13:05

Attachment Modes

Center	On
End Point	On
Intersect	On
Midpoint	On
Node Point	On
Perpendicular	On
Quadrant	On
Tangent	On

Attach Mode	Off

OK		Cancel

(Untitled)

2. Move the pointer to highlight the boxes within the dialogue box.

You can switch the current setting by highlighting the box and selecting it. This type of box turns a feature of AutoSketch on or off. When you change back and forth between values by pressing your pick button, you toggle the AutoSketch tools.

Since you aren't going to change any values in this dialogue box, you are ready to exit.

3. Move the arrow to the Cancel box at the bottom of the dialogue box and select it.

AutoSketch will roll back the dialogue box. Selecting the Cancel box closes the dialogue box without changing any values even if you have typed information or made new selections. To close the box and activate any changes you make, you would select the OK box. If the information you entered won't work, you will see a warning message. You must select OK or Cancel to close the dialogue box before selecting another menu, command, or drawing element.

Ending Your Drawing Session

When you are ready to stop drawing, you need to tell AutoSketch that you are ending the session you began when you loaded the program. In this unit, you have been practicing the basics of AutoSketch. For now, you can stop drawing without worrying about saving your drawings.

1. Select the **File** menu and the **Quit** command.

A dialogue box will be displayed, warning you that you are trying to quit drawing without saving your work.

2. Select **Discard**.

This time you can select Discard since you don't want to keep your practice drawing. The screen should look the way it did when you sat down at the workstation to load AutoSketch.

Key Terms

menu	rubber band
arrow pointer	drawing units
pick button	hand pointer
Insert key	crosses/window box
outlining block	dialogue box
pulldown menu	toggle
Scroll bar	

Let's Review

 *Questions*

1. How can you select menu items, pulldown menus, or drawing locations?

   _____

   _____

   _____

2. When you are using a mouse as a pointing device, how do you indicate a selection to the computer?

   _____

   _____

3. What do the numbers in the upper right corner of the menu bar mean?

   _____

   _____

   _____

4. When you move the mouse or digitizer around, what does this movement control on the screen?

   _____

   _____

   _____

5. What keys can be used in place of a mouse or digitizer to select items on the screen?

   _____

   _____

6. How do you enter relative and polar coordinates using AutoSketch?

   _____

   _____

7. What does the arrow pointer become when used to select drawing elements for editing?

   _____

8. What feature can be used to select several drawing elements at a time for editing?

_____

_____

9. What is the name of the box used to change several drawing settings at one time?

_____

_____

10. What menu and command do you use to end a drawing session?

_____

Problems

Use the Polygon command to create each of the drawings below.

1. Enter the absolute coordinates listed below to draw a figure.

Starting point:	2,2	Point 5:	2,8
Point 1:	7,1	Point 6:	3,6
Point 2:	9,3	Point 7:	1,4
Point 3:	4,5	Point 8:	4,3
Point 4:	11,7	Point 9:	2,2

2. Use the polar coordinates listed below to draw a figure.

Starting point:	5,2
Point 1:	P(5,0)
Point 2:	P(3,90)
Point 3:	P(2.75,120)
Point 4:	P(4.34,213)
Point 5:	P(3,270)

3. Use the relative coordinates listed below to create a letter of the alphabet. Before you begin, can you guess what the letter will be?

Starting point:	3,3	Point 7:	R(-2,0)
Point 1:	R(4,0)	Point 8:	R(0,1)
Point 2:	R(0,1)	Point 9:	R(3,0)
Point 3:	R(-3,0)	Point 10:	R(0,1)
Point 4:	R(0,1)	Point 11:	R(-4,0)
Point 5:	R(2,0)	Point 12:	R(0,-5)
Point 6:	R(0,1)		

4. Use all three coordinate systems listed below to draw a figure. The coordinates listed have two starting points.

First Starting point:	11,1	Second Starting point:	9,1
Point 1:	R(0,3)	Point 1:	R(0,3)
Point 2:	P(4.23,135)	Point 2:	P(-2,0)
Point 3:	R(-3,-3)	Point 3:	R(0,-3)
Point 4:	5,1	Point 4:	7,1
Point 5:	R(6,0)		

Extend Your Knowledge

1. Use grid paper to make a freehand drawing with the coordinates listed below. Assume that the lower left corner of the paper is 0,0.

Starting Point:	5,5
Point 1:	R(0,4)
Point 2:	P(2,45)
Point 3:	P(2,-45)
Point 4:	R(0,-4)
Point 5:	5,5

2. As a project, develop a drawing of a familiar object. Make three sets of coordinate values for the drawing. One set will use absolute coordinates, one set will use relative coordinates, and one set will use polar coordinates. Select three classmates. Give each classmate a different set of coordinates to draw. After they have completed their drawings, compare the drawings. Do all three drawings look the same? Why or why not?

UNIT 6

The Draw Menu

Objectives:

■ *To draw basic shapes.*

■ *To understand the use of the Alt, Ctrl, and function keys.*

■ *To add text to your drawings.*

The Draw menu is used to create a drawing. You will use the Draw commands to complete the exercises in the rest of this text. This menu opens up to you the possibilities of CAD. Using these commands, you can place points anywhere on the screen and later refer back to them. You can locate lines, circles, and arcs. You can draw a box simply by picking starting and ending points. You can even place words on a drawing.

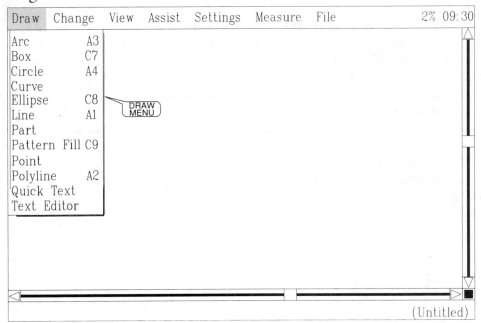

All of the Draw menu commands, as well as other menu commands, can be selected by using the arrow pointer.

The Alternate, Control, and Function Keys

AutoSketch®
Reference
Manual
p. 95

You can also select some of the commands on the Draw menu by holding down the *Alt* (Alternate) *key* and pressing one of the numbered *function keys.* An example of a function key is the **F1** key. This shortcut for choosing a command is shown on a pulldown menu to the right of the command. For example, the A1 next to Line means that you could hold down the Alt key and press the F1 key to activate the command. You can also select some commands on other menus by striking only a function key.

Another way to select commands is by holding down the *Ctrl* (Control) *key* and pressing a function key. For example, C7 (on the Draw menu) means that you can select the box command by using the Ctrl and F7 function keys. With these shortcuts, you can change from one command to another without pulling down a menu. You will practice using these keys in this unit. As you learn how to use them, you will become quicker at making drawings with AutoSketch.

The Line Command

p. 107

You practiced drawing lines in Unit 5. To learn more about the Line command, use the following steps to draw the line shown to the right:

1. Load AutoSketch.
2. Press the **Alt** key and the **F1** key to select the **Line** command.

▶ *Hint:*

Remember that the command prompt in the lower left corner of your screen area (below the open screen border) will let you know what sequence AutoSketch expects you to follow when giving commands. You can use this prompt to figure out what you should do next as you draw. The first word in the prompt is always the command you are using.

3. Enter the coordinates **2,2**.
4. To finish the straight line across the bottom of the screen, enter coordinates **6,2**.

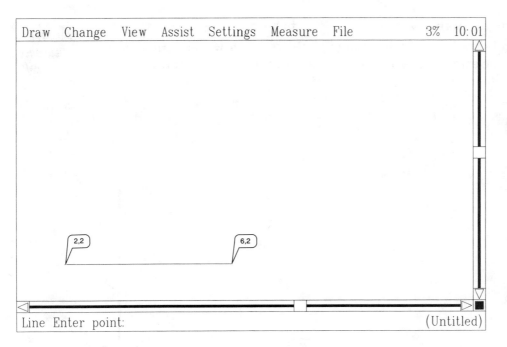

```
Draw  Change  View  Assist  Settings  Measure  File          3%   10:01
```

```
┌─2,2                          ┌─6,2
```

Line Enter point: (Untitled)

5. Make several more lines on the screen, each connected to the previous line.

▶ ***Hint:***

To connect a line to the line before, either enter the last coordinates of points on the keyboard, or use your pointing device. To use the pointing device, press the pick button twice at the last point.

6. To clear the screen, pull down the **Change** menu and use the **Erase** command to remove the lines. (Remember, you can use the crosses/window feature to speed up the process.)

Erasing is one way to clear the drawing area when you have filled the space and don't want to store the drawing.

Now let's try drawing a shape.

1. Draw a square using the **Line** command.

▶ ***Hint:***

For help in drawing equal sides, select the Assist Menu and the Grid command. If you are having trouble drawing completely straight lines, select the Assist menu and the Ortho command. With Ortho, you can draw lines that are straight across or straight up and down.

*AutoSketch®
Reference
Manual*

p. 78
pp. 141-
143

pp.96-98
pp. 119-
122

2. Then draw another square around the first one.

Your drawing should look something like the one below. The squares may not be the same size or in the same location as they are in the illustration.

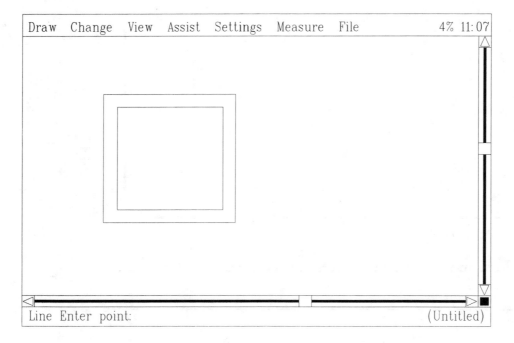

The Box Command

The Box command allows you to draw boxes around or inside objects without having to make all the sides equal. AutoSketch automatically creates boxes when you use this command. The only information AutoSketch needs is two points that establish the size. To practice using this command, follow these steps:

1. Select the **Box** command.
2. Select a point within the smaller of the two squares you have just drawn.

This point is one corner of the box.

3. Move the pointer diagonally to see the boxes that you can draw.

When you use this command, you can see the box on the screen before you actually add it to your drawing. AutoSketch lets you experiment with the size and position of the element before choosing the way it will look in the drawing.

This method of selecting where you want an object placed in a drawing and how big you want it to be is called *dragging*. Boxes, circles, and arcs are examples of elements that are dragged into position. Some elements that are being dragged are shown on the screen with jagged lines. When you tell AutoSketch where and what size you want the object, the jagged lines are replaced with smooth ones.

4. When the box is the size you want, pick another point to select the opposite corner.

pp. 18-19

AutoSketch will create a box with the dimensions you have selected. Your drawing should look something like the one below.

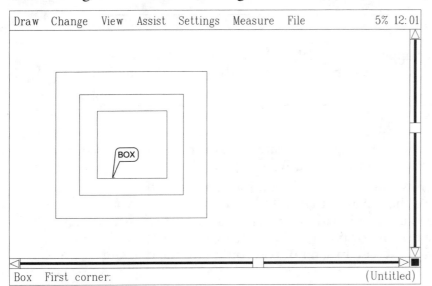

Saving Your Drawings

When you have made a new drawing and have decided to keep it, you need to instruct AutoSketch to save it. After a drawing is saved, you can view it again, edit it, and plot it (produce a paper copy of it). Let's save this practice drawing to learn the save process.

pp. 67-69
p. 80
p. 177

1. Select the **File** menu and the **Save As** command.

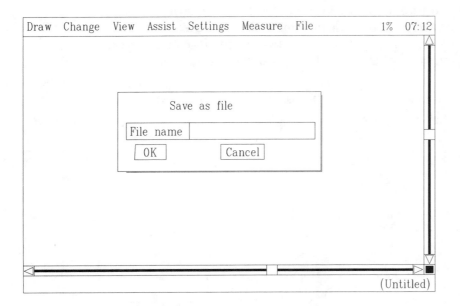

A dialogue box will be displayed on the screen. AutoSketch needs to know the name under which you want the drawing stored. For AutoSketch, *file* is another name for a drawing. The name of the drawing can use letters, numerals, and the symbols such as $, -, or _. The name can be up to eight spaces long.

AutoSketch®
Reference
Manual

2. Move the pointer until the empty box next to Filename is highlighted and type a name for your drawing. Let's use **BOXES**.

▶ *Hint:*

> You can enter either uppercase (capital) or lowercase letters or both. If you make a mistake in typing, press the Backspace key to erase.

3. Close the dialogue box.

What happened to the label "Untitled"? It should have changed to "BOXES." This drawing is now on file in AutoSketch.

Save all the drawings you create in this text for exercises and problems. You can give them names that will help you remember what is in them. You can also use combinations of letters and numbers that will remind you of the exercise or problem for which you drew them. For example, for the first exercise in Unit 6, you could save the drawing as E6-1.

You now have the drawing BOXES stored, but it is still displayed on the screen. How do you start another drawing?

4. Select the **File** menu and the **New** command.

p. 118

You should see a clear drawing area with the label "Untitled" in the lower right corner. From now on, clear the screen whenever you choose.

5. Draw three more boxes.

6. Without saving this drawing, pull down the **File** menu and select the **New** command.

What happens? If you forget to use the Save command to store a new drawing, AutoSketch warns you by displaying a dialogue box. If you choose the Save option from this box, you can store the drawing. If you don't want to keep the drawing, discard it, or cancel to continue drawing.

7. Since you drew this second group of boxes just to learn about saving, pick **Discard**.

AutoSketch®
Reference
Manual

✔✔ *Exercise 1*

1. Use the Line command to draw a triangle, using the coordinates
    listed.

    Point 1: 4,2   To Point 3: 6,5

    To Point 2: 8,2   To close the triangle: 4,2

2. Draw a box around the triangle.

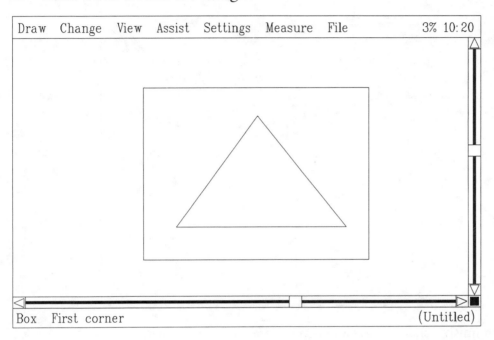

The Polyline Command

The Polyline command is used to create a shape (closed or open) made with a series of connected lines. This command joins lines end to end as you draw from one point to the next.

A closed shape made with a series of connected lines is a *polygon*. With the Polyline command, you can use line segments to make polygons such as triangles (three sides), hexagons (six sides), and octagons (eight sides).

p. 158

▶ *Hint:*

Since this command is used so often in drawing, selecting it with the Alt and F2 keys will save you time.

1. Select the **Polyline** command.
2. Draw the top shape from the illustration below.

When you return to your starting point, AutoSketch recognizes that the shape is complete and finishes the object.

When you want to leave a shape open, select the last point twice.

3. Now draw the bottom shape.

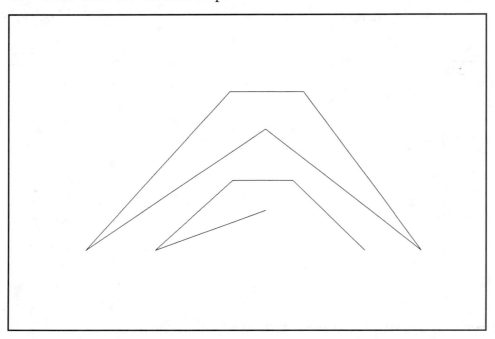

After you finish a shape, you can keep on drawing objects without having to select the command again; the prompt "Polyline First point:" appears in the left corner of the screen.

It is easier to draw a shape by using this command than by using the Line command. You don't have to keep pressing the pick button or Insert key to tell AutoSketch that you want to use the last point you entered as the starting point for the next line.

4. Select the **Change** menu and the **Erase** command and erase one side of the top shape.

What happens to the rest of the shape?

When you want to change what you have drawn, AutoSketch treats a shape drawn with the Polyline command differently from one drawn with the Line command. When you erase, the shape is viewed as a single object, even if it is a series of lines that aren't closed to form a finished shape. If you erase one of the line segments, the entire object will disappear.

*AutoSketch®
Reference
Manual*

pp. 63-64

✔✔ *Exercise 2*

Draw a shape like the one below. Use 3,1 as the starting point.

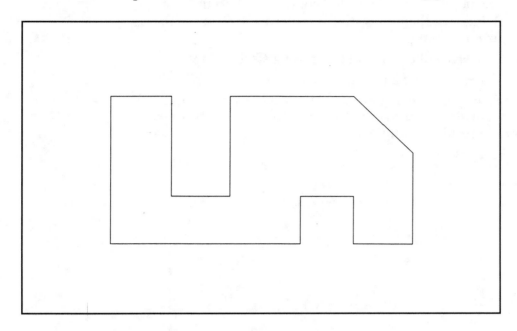

✔✔ *Exercise 3*

Use the Polyline command to make the drawing below.

The Pattern Fill Command

*AutoSketch®
Reference
Manual*
p. 129

The Pattern Fill command is similar to the Polyline command, because you construct a series of lines that connect back to the first point. The enclosed area then fills with the pattern and shade of the color you are currently using.

1.   Select the **Pattern Fill** command by pressing **Ctrl** and **F9**.

2.   Draw the shape from the illustration below.

When you return to your starting point, watch what happens to the enclosed area. Autosketch knows that you have completed the object. The object should be filled with the pattern shown below.

3. Select the **Accept** box.

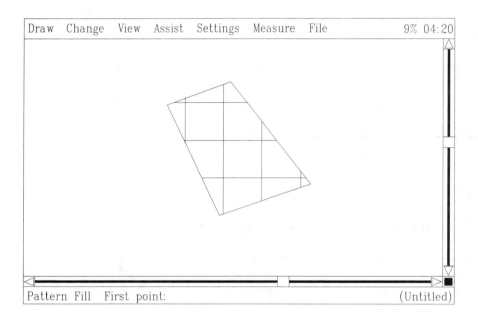

AutoSketch treats the fill region like any other Polyline. Touching any part of the fill region affects the entire object.

3. Erase the fill region by using a crosses box.

Did the whole object erase or only the part within the crosses box?

The Point Command

The Point command makes a dot on the drawing area for you to use as a reference. Reference points can be used to locate the beginning of a line or arc or the center of a circle. You also could use this command to tell AutoSketch the exact location where you want to attach another shape to your drawing. The Node Point option of the Attach command from the Settings Menu is used to add the shapes. Points can also help you when you learn how to measure distances and figure bearings (directions) between objects. This is done with the measurement and the Point command.

**pp. 156 -
157**

pp. 10-17

You will learn to use the reference points in later units. For now, try adding some points to your BOXES drawing. To do this, you must first open the BOXES drawing.

Opening a Drawing

AutoSketch®
Reference
Manual

p. 119

1.   To tell AutoSketch to display BOXES, select the **File** menu and the **Open** command.

Using this command is just like opening a drawer in which you've stored all your drawings. You will see a dialogue box that displays icons, or small pictures, of stored drawings.

2.   Move the pointer until the **BOXES** icon is highlighted and select it.

To view your entire list of AutoSketch drawings, use the scroll bar to the right. Pick the arrow to move one drawing at a time. Select the open box to move several drawings.

▶ *Hint:*

You could also move the pointer so that the empty box next to File is highlighted, type the name, and select OK or press the Enter key.

3. Close the dialogue box.

Your BOXES drawing should be displayed on the screen.

4.   Select the **Point** command.

5.   Draw points in the center of the box and in the middle of each side of the largest square. (Don't worry about finding the exact centers.)

Small dots will appear on the screen.

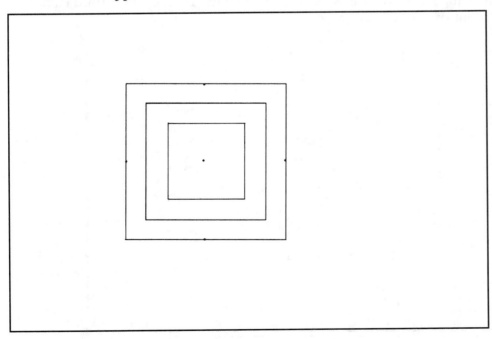

The Circle Command

The Line, Box, Polyline, and Point commands use points and lines to make drawings. The next group of Draw commands uses circles and curves. They are interesting to use because they help make drawing faster.

First, let's try drawing a circle.

1. Select the **Circle** command.

▶ *Hint:*

Pressing the Alt key and the F4 key activates Circle. The prompt "Circle Center point:" will appear.

2. Pick a point for the center of the circle.
3. Move the pointer away from the center point.

What do you see on the screen?

You can move the edge of the circle back and forth to increase or decrease its size. Dragging the edge allows you to select the size of circle you want. Notice that this edge looks rather rough.

4. When you decide how big to make the circle, select the second point.

AutoSketch will draw a smooth circle.

ᨆᨆᨆᨆᨆ *Exercise 4*

Make a drawing with two circles like the one below. Then create a third circle with a center point of your choice.

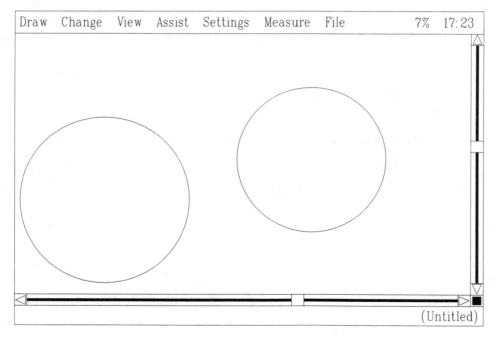

Circle 1: Center point 3,4
Circle 2: Center point 8,5

The Arc Command

An *arc* is part of a circle. To draw an arc, you need to pick three points:

- the starting point for the arc
- a point on the arc
- the ending point for the arc.

1. Select the **Arc** command.

**AutoSketch®
Reference
Manual**

pp.4-6

▶ *Hint:*

Use the Alt and F3 keys as a shortcut.

The prompt "Arc Start point" will be displayed.

2. Select the first point.
3. Then pick a point on the arc.

This point tells AutoSketch the size of the circle that the arc you want to draw is a part of.

After you have selected the first and second points, you can drag the arc into place until it is the length you want.

4. Pick the third point to draw the arc smoothly.

✔✔✔✔✔ *Exercise 5*

Draw a radio tower like the one below, using the Arc and Polyline commands.

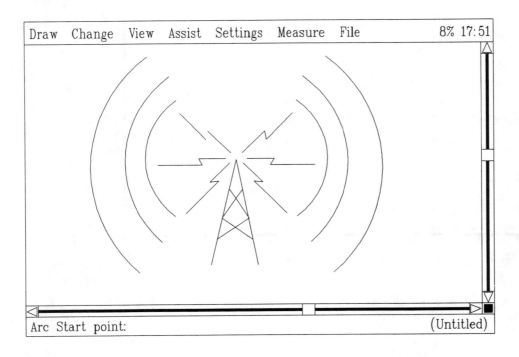

The Curve Command

AutoSketch®
Reference
Manual

pp. 50-53

The powerful Curve command takes information about the lines you enter and replaces straight line segments with a smooth, curved line. The points that show the beginning and ending of the straight lines are called *control points*. The lines set up a *frame* for the curve. AutoSketch fits a curve to the frame formed by the control points.

The closer you place the control points to one another, the smoother the curve will be when you are finished. AutoSketch actually passes the curve through the first and last control points (unless the curve is closed) and pulls it toward the other control points. When you place control points closer together in one part of the curve, you will exert more pull on that part. The more control points you use, the closer the curve will fit the desired frame and the longer it will take AutoSketch to calculate the curve line. The curve cannot have more than 100 control points.

1. Select the **Curve** command.
2. Enter these coordinates for control points:

    1,2

    3,3

    4,6

    5,2

    6,6

The curve frame should look like the one below.

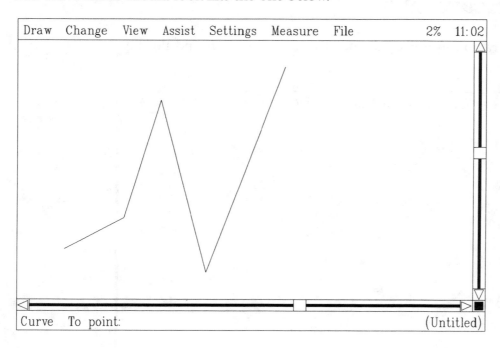

AutoSketch®
Reference
Manual

3. To draw the curve, enter coordinates for the last point again. You should see a curve like the one on the screen below.

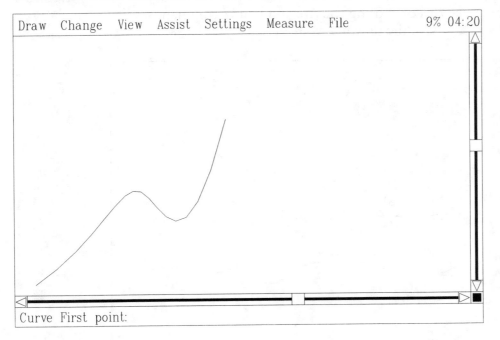

| Draw   Change   View   Assist   Settings   Measure   File   9% 04:20 |

Curve First point:

▶ *Hint:*

When you want to draw a closed curve, return to your starting point and pick it again

You can see the frame for a curve you have drawn by selecting the Frame Option on the Assist menu (Unit 9) or the Curve option on the Settings menu (Unit 10). To erase a curve, pick a point on the frame and select it. If you pick a point on the curve, it will not erase. You can also use a crosses or window box.

pp. 50-53
pp. 93-95

AutoSketch®
Reference
Manual

⌄⌄⌄⌄⌄ *Exercise 6*

Draw a boat like this one, using the Arc and Curve commands. Add a second sail, and save the drawing as BOAT.

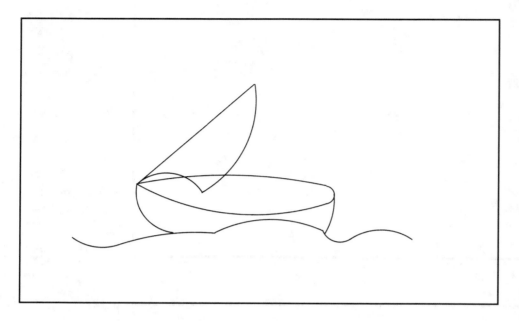

The Ellipse Command

An ellipse looks like a flattened circle. It has a center point and two axes. The two axes intersect at the center point of the ellipse and are 90° apart.

With AutoSketch, there are three ways to draw an ellipse. In this unit, you will learn one way. With this method, you choose the center point of the ellipse and each axis.

pp. 72-77

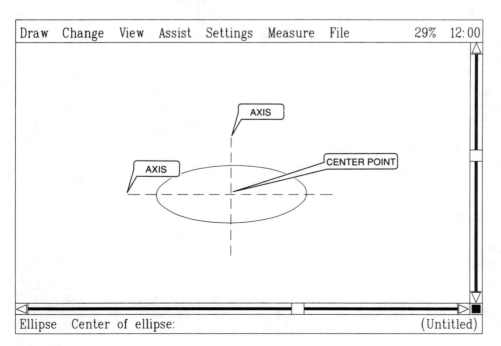

Center Point and Both Axes

1. Select the **Ellipse** command.
2. Select a point on the screen for the center point.
3. Select another point on the screen.

This is the axis endpoint (the point where the first axis will end).

4. Move the pointing device around the screen.

You will see an ellipse that changes shape as you move the next point.

5. Select a point for the other axis distance.

AutoSketch®
Reference
Manual
pp. 72 - 77

The Quick Text Command

The Quick Text command on the Draw menu allows you to add lettering, dimensions, and notes to your drawings. Text is one of the most useful commands in AutoSketch. It makes letters and numbers that are a set size and shape, are a set distance apart, and are shown in a certain position.

pp. 192-
194

1. To practice adding text, pull out the drawing you made for Exercise 1 in this chapter.
2. Select the Quick Text command.

The prompt "Text Enter point:" will appear.

3. Select a point in an empty area of the screen for the text to start.

An underline cursor will appear in the drawing area at the point you selected. The lower left end of the line of text will be at this cursor. AutoSketch will prompt you to enter the text.

4. Type the letters in your first and last name.

You will see the characters appear on the screen. If you make a mistake, press the Backspace key to erase the letters and type the correct characters.

5. Press the pick button. (If the keyboard is your only pointing device, hold the **Ctrl** (Control) key and press the **J** key.

The underline cursor should move to the next line.

6. On the next two lines, write your address.
7. When you are finished entering all the text, press the **Enter** key.

When you use the Quick Text command, each line you create is treated as a single entity. This means that when you erase, one line is erased at a time.

8. Press **F1**.

One line of your address disappears.

9. Press **F1** again.

In addition to letters and numbers, you can also use special characters in text for a drawing or place lines over or under text. To enter these characters, use the percent sign (%) and the symbols listed below to signal where these characters should begin and end:

%%o – Overscore (line over character)

%%u – Underscore (line under character)

%%d – Degree symbol (°)

%%p – Plus/minus tolerance symbol (±)

%%c – Diameter dimensioning symbol (Ø)

%%% – Percent symbol (%)

These control sequences are entered right along with the text to "turn on" and "turn off" the characters, underlining, or overlining. For example, to add the dimension 45°, type 45%%d%%D on the keyboard.

▶ *Hint:*

Because the underscore and the overscore are turned off automatically at the end of each line of text, you must reenter the control sequence each time you need to use these features.

10. On a new line of text, type **%%uTRIANGLE IN BOX%%u** to write a name on your drawing and underline it.

Exercise 7

Make a drawing like the one below, and add the text.

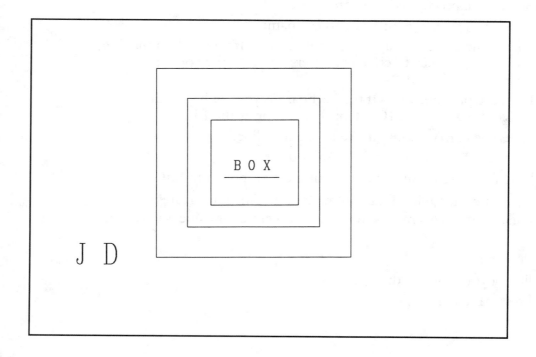

The Text Editor

Another way to add text is with the Text Editor. This command has several options that make it more powerful than the Quick Text command.

1. Select the **Text Editor** command.
2. Pick a point on the drawing where you want the text to start.

A dialogue box appears.

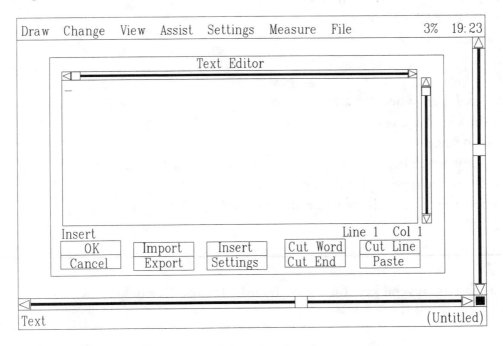

3. Type in the text you want to add to the drawing.
4. Select **OK**.

The text will appear on the drawing.

Erasing Text

Each time you add text with the Text Editor, the line or lines of text will be treated as one entity.

1. Select the **Text Editor** command and pick a point on the screen.
2. Add a line of text and press **ENTER**.
3. Add several more lines of text. Press enter after each line.
4. Select **OK**.
5. Press the **F1** key to erase.

How many lines disappeared at once?

▶ *Hint:*

To bring back text you have erased, press the F2 key (Undo).

Editing Text

If you make a mistake while entering text in the Text Editor dialogue box, you can use the choices in the box to make corrections. If you enter a long section of text, this is much faster than backspacing.

1. Select the **Text Editor** command and pick a point on the screen.
2. Type several lines of text.
3. Press the pick button at the first letter of a word.
4. Select the **Cut Word** box.

The word disappears.

5. Select **Paste**.

The word reappears.

6. Select a point anywhere on a line of text.
7. Select the **Cut Line** box.

The line disappears.

8. Pick a point at the beginning of the text. Select the **Paste** box.

The line that was cut appears in this new place.

9. Pick a point in the middle of a line and try the **Cut End** box.

What happens?

▶ *Hint:*

You can also use several keys on the keyboard. Try the Delete key, the Backspace key, and the space bar.

Importing Text

The Import option allows you to bring in text from an outside source such as a word processor. Some of the common word processing software programs are Wordperfect®, PFS®, Microsoft Word®, and MultiMate®. If you have such a program, you may follow the steps below to try out this option. Keep in mind that the word processor used must be in a DOS format. You may also import text created in an ASCII format. You can use the line editor of your DOS-based computer to create this type of text. (Refer to your DOS manual for an explanation of the line editor, which uses EDLIN commands.)

1. From an outside source described above, create the following text:

THIS IS AN IMPORT TEXT TEST

one

two two

three three three

four four four four

five five five five five

six six six six six six

This concludes the test.

2. Once you have created this text, save it as an ASCII file.

> ▶ *Hint:*
>
> You may need to read the reference manual for the word processor you are using. Keep a record of the file location (drive and directory location). Refer to Appendix A for a discussion of DOS-related topics such as directories and files.

3. Load AutoSketch.
4. Select **Text Editor** from the **Draw** menu.
5. Select an insertion point.
6. Select the **Import** option.

A dialogue box appears called "Import a File."

7. Type in the drive, subdirectory, and file name of the text file you completed earlier.
8. Select **OK** to close the Text Editor.

Your text should appear on the AutoSketch screen.

Exporting Text

The Export option allows you to send text from a drawing to a file outside of AutoSketch. You might send it to another software program such as a word processor described above.

1. Load AutoSketch and select the **Text Editor** command from the **Draw** menu.
2. Create the following text:

    THIS IS AN EXPORT TEXT TEST

    six six six six six six

    five five five five five

    four four four four

    three three three

    two two

    one

    This concludes the test.

3. Select the **Export** option.

A dialogue box appears called "Export a File."

4. Type in the drive, subdirectory, and an existing file you would like the file to be stored under. For example, type C:\SKETCH3\EXPORT.TST.

If you use the example given, the text will be stored in the C drive, in the SKETCH3 directory, and in a file named EXPORT.TST.

5. Select **OK** to close the dialogue box.

AutoSketch will load the text into a file in ASCII form. You should now be able to load the file into your word processor. Because the file is in ASCII, properties such as color and font will not be exported.

You may have noticed several other choices on the Text Editor dialogue box. The same dialogue box appears when you select this command from the Change menu. You will learn to use these selections in Unit 7.

The Part Command

*AutoSketch®
Reference
Manual*

**pp. 124 -
125**

The Part command helps you create drawings because it allows you to use shapes, figures, designs, and whole drawings that you have stored and insert them into a new drawing.

Let's try out this command.

1. Start a new drawing.

2. Now select the **Part** command.

When you select this command from the Draw menu, a Select Part File dialogue box like the one at the next page appears in the center of the drawing area.

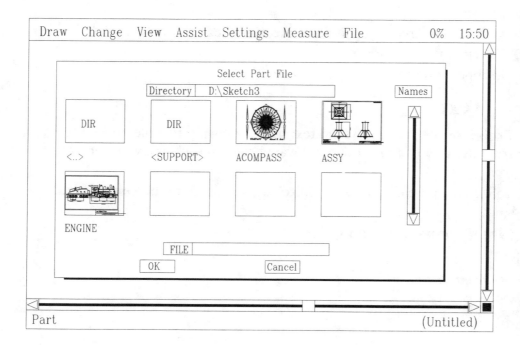

Use this box to indicate which finished AutoSketch drawing you want to add to the drawing you are currently making. The drawings that you have saved are listed in the directory (group of drawings) shown in the box. The drawings are listed by name and by icon. An icon is a small drawing that looks like the actual drawing.

3. To select a file to add to the new drawing, move the pointer until the BOAT icon is highlighted and pick it. (Or highlight the box labeled **File**, type **BOAT**, and select the **OK** box to the right of the drawing name.)

▶ *Note:*

The BOAT drawing was created earlier. If you do not have this drawing stored, pick another icon. Your boat drawing may be stored, but does not appear. If so pick the arrow to the right. A new icon is displayed. Continue until you have seen all the icons.

4. Close the dialogue box by picking **OK.**

When you close the box, the part file you have chosen will appear on the drawing area. The base point, which is called the *part insertion base,* of the drawing will be placed at the current location of the arrow pointer in the new drawing.

5. Move the arrow pointer to drag the part into place.

6. Press your pick button.

AutoSketch will add the part to the drawing.

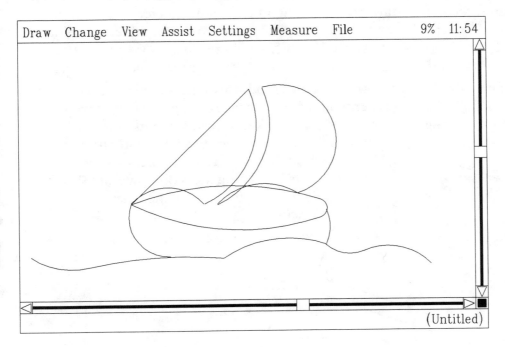

7. Try adding something to the drawing, such as a cloud.

✔✔ *Exercise 8*

Several drawings are supplied with AutoSketch. Use the Part command to select some of the drawings. Use them as parts to create a new drawing. If you don't see these drawings listed when you use the Part command, see the Open command, page 193, for how to find them.

Key Terms

Alt key	function keys	dragging
file	polygon	arc
control points	frame	part insertion base
	Ctrl Key	ellipse

Young Writers and Illustrators Learn AutoSketch

The stories on this page were written and illustrated by second grade students. Both stories and drawings were done entirely with AutoSketch.

The stories featured here were done in an art class taught by Paula Passante. Paula begins the initial AutoSketch training in class. Students receive additional training during Saturday workshops. Workshops are led by computer coordinator Ken Ford, who is assisted by Grace Vento-Zogby, a reading coordinator. After the Saturday workshops, students are able to use their time more efficiently in class.

These types of activities provide an authentic learning experience, according to Grace. Especially exciting is her work with remedial reading students, which includes some of the authors featured here. Experienced students go on to help younger students write and illustrate stories with AutoSketch. Grace also supports classroom teachers by sharing ideas on how AutoSketch can serve as a tool to enhance the curriculum.

Let's Review

 *Questions*

1. Name three keys that can be used to select commands.

    _____

    _____

    _____

2. What information can you find out from the command prompt in the lower left corner of the screen?

    _____

    _____

3. How can you draw connected lines using the Line command?

    _____

4. Explain how to use the Box command.

    _____

    _____

5. What is one advantage of drawing a shape using the Polyline command?

    _____

6. What happens if you erase one line segment of a Polyline?

    _____

7. How is the Fill Region command similar to the Polyline command?

    _____

    _____

8. Name three uses of points entered with the Point command.

    _____

    _____

9. What two points do you enter when drawing a circle?

_____

_____

10. What three points do you enter when drawing an arc?

_____

_____

11. How does AutoSketch draw a curve?

_____

_____

_____

12. How do you enter underlining in text for a drawing?

_____

13. Where is a part file placed in a new drawing?

_____

_____

Extend Your Knowledge

1. Make a freehand drawing of a boat similar to the one shown in this unit. Keep track of the time it takes you to make the drawing, and compare to the time it takes you to draw the boat with AutoSketch.

2. Use grid paper to draw the floor plan of your bedroom, as if you were looking down from above. Let each square represent 1'. Show the shape and location of your bedroom furniture, door, and window. Keep this drawing for future use.

3. Draw a halloween-type mask on grid paper. Keep it simple. Recreate the mask on the screen with AutoSketch.

The Change Menu

Objectives:
- To correct drawing mistakes.
- To change the size or shape of drawing elements.
- To move elements around within a drawing.
- To change text on a drawing.

When you make a drawing, you use drawing elements like lines, circles, and polygons. You often include text and sometimes add measurements to the drawing to show sizes. With the Change Menu, you can edit the drawing elements as you like.

Draw	Change	View	Assist	Settings	Measure	File	1%	20:00

Undo	F1
Redo	F2
Group	A9
Ungroup	A10
Box Array	C2
Break	F4
Chamfer	
Copy	F6
Erase	F3
Fillet	
Mirror	C3
Move	F5
Property	
Ring Array	C4
Rotate	C5
Scale	C6
Stretch	F7
Text Editor	

(Untitled)

Why do you need the change menu? Many times in the drawing process, you make mistakes that you want to erase. Or maybe you have added extra lines to the drawing for measurement purposes and need to remove them to finish the drawing.

You are already familiar with a pencil eraser and how it works. With the eraser, you can erase a part of a line or an entire object. You can change the colors in a drawing, the position of shapes, or even the size of elements, but many of those changes are hard to make by ordinary erasing.

When you use CAD, the pencil eraser seems like a Stone Age tool. The Change menu of AutoSketch is probably the most effective and efficient part of the program because you can change a drawing easily. When you know how to apply the Change commands, you can edit your drawings quickly. The Change commands are as important in producing drawings as the Draw commands.

You can see on the menu that several of the Change commands can be selected by using the Alternate, Control, and/or Function keys. Using these keys is a shortcut method for activating the commands.

As you learned in Unit 5, when you select one of these commands, the arrow pointer changes to a hand pointer. AutoSketch uses the hand pointer to remind you that you are editing a drawing instead of creating one.

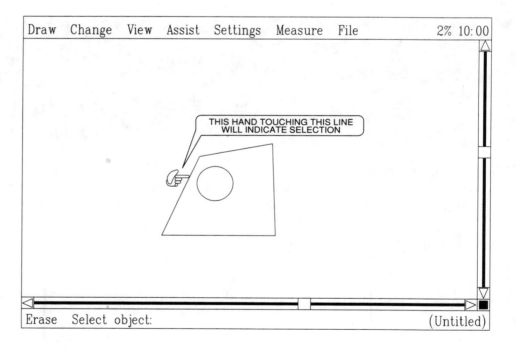

The Erase Command

The Erase option makes changes and corrections easy. You can erase any drawing element, including text.

**AutoSketch®
Reference
Manual**

p. 78

▶ *Hint:*

You can activate the Erase command just by pressing the F3 key.

✔✔ *Exercise 1*

To review how the Erase command works, load AutoSketch and draw a bird house. Then erase the side and bottom lines.

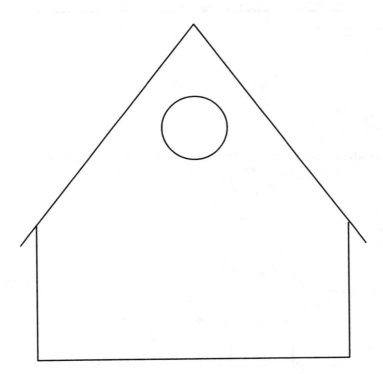

Selecting individual lines for erasing is fun, but would you find erasing a complete drawing with 30 or 40 lines enjoyable? You probably would not. In this case, you could create a crosses or window box, as shown on the next page, to surround the entire drawing. Then you could quickly remove all the drawing elements.

▶ *Hint:*

Surrounding an object with a box also helps when you can't easily line up the hand pointer with the object selected for erasing or other editing.

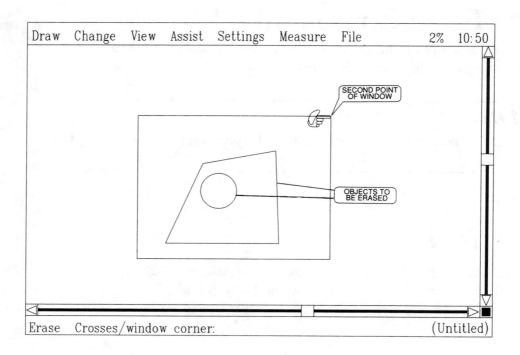

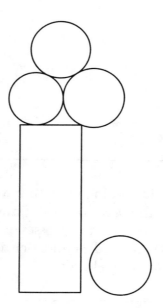

✔✔✔✔✔ *Exercise 2*

To review using a window box to erase, draw the five elements shown below and then erase three of them using a window. Then erase the other two by using the crosses box.

The Break Command

AutoSketch®
Reference
Manual

pp. 27 - 31

The Break command is also used to erase, but it is designed to let you remove only part of a drawing element. It trims the drawing parts rather than completely removing an entire drawing element. Refer to the illustration as you follow the numbered steps below.

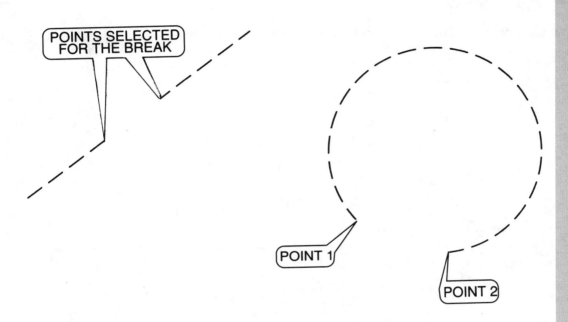

1. Draw a line and a circle.
2. Select the **Break** command.

▶ *Hint:*

You can use the F4 key to activate this command without pulling down the Change menu.

3. Select the line.

What happens? The solid line you drew should now be dotted, and the hand pointer should have changed back to an arrow pointer.

4. Select two points on the line, one for the opening of the break and one for the closing.

There should be two shorter lines on your screen instead of one longer line. The middle of your original line should have disappeared.

5. Now select the circle.
6. Change it into an arc by selecting two break points.

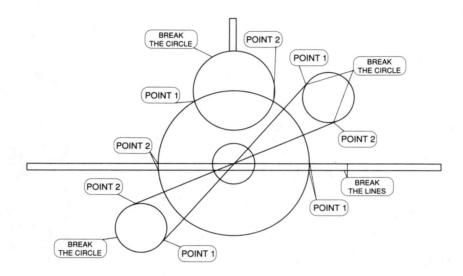

AutoSketch®
Reference
Manual

> ▶ *Hint:*
>
> Always select points in a **counterclockwise** direction to cut out part of a circle. AutoSketch will redraw an arc from the part not broken out of the circle.

✔✔✔✔✔ *Exercise 3*

Draw the circle and lines below and make breaks in the locations shown.

The Undo Command

Maybe you have noticed the Undo command on the menu and wondered how it is different from the Erase command. If you think that the Undo command eliminates something from a drawing, you are right! However, instead of removing elements you select, it undoes the result of the last command you gave to AutoSketch. If you drew some lines and then erased them, you could use the Undo command to make those lines reappear in your drawing. When drawing, you can make mistakes or change your mind without ruining your work.

Whenever you want to step back one operation in your drawing or editing process, simply select the Undo command. It removes elements from a drawing in reverse order to which you drew them.

pp. 209 -
210

▶ *Hint:*

To use Undo, select it from the Change menu or press the F1 key.

✔✔ *Exercise 4*

Draw circles and lines shown below. Next, add the text "Telephone Receiver." Then undo each of the features.

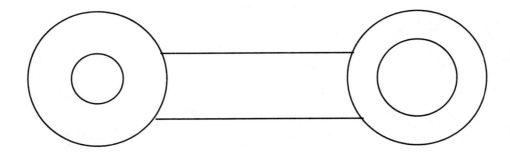

The Redo Command

p. 167

What if you get carried away with the use of the Undo command and discover that you have undone more than you should have? There is a way to reverse the Undo command—the Redo command. This command exists because you aren't the only one to want to change your mind about undoing.

The Redo command is easy to use, but it doesn't work unless you have previously used the Undo command. To activate the Redo command, simply select it from the menu or press the F2 key. The last object you removed from the drawing by using the Undo command will reappear.

✓✓✓✓✓ *Exercise 5*

AutoSketch®
Reference
Manual

Use lines and arcs to draw the hammer shown below. Erase two of the lines, undo the erasing for one line, and then redo the erasing for the line.

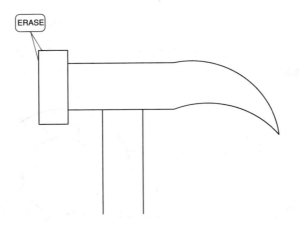

The Group Command

The Group command speeds up the editing process. It makes it easier to manipulate the drawing elements and improves the performance of your CAD workstation. With the Group command, you can select drawing elements and cement them together to form a *group*. After they have been grouped, they will all respond together when any one of them is influenced by the action of any command.

pp. 98 - 100

For instance, suppose you decide to erase one element that is connected to a group of drawing elements. If the single element is selected with the hand pointer, all the grouped elements will be erased.

1. First use the **Draw** menu to make a drawing with six elements (like lines, boxes, polygons, or circles).

2. Then select the **Group** command.

▶ *Hint:*

Try using the Alt key and the F9 key as a quick way to activate this command.

The command prompt "Group Select object" will appear.

► *Hint:*

If you want to use a crosses or window box instead of selecting objects one by one, press your select button again to get the prompt "Group Crosses/window corner."

3. Use your pointing device to indicate two elements of your drawing that you want to group.

What happens to the elements that you selected? They should be shown in dotted lines. AutoSketch will keep prompting you to add objects to the group until you select the Group command again or a different command.

4. Select the **Group** command to finish forming this group.

5. Erase one of the two elements you have grouped.

   Both elements disappear together. You can also use the Group command with other commands for moving and copying groups of elements. You will learn more about these commands later in this Unit.

6. Group three of the remaining objects.

   Suppose you wanted to trim away part of one of the elements in the group.

7. Select the **Break** command and the break points.

   Does the command work? You should have discovered that you can't break objects that have been grouped.

   What if you want to add more drawing elements to a group you set up previously?

8. Add another element to the drawing.

9. Then use the **Group** command to select the elements you grouped in step 6 and the element you just drew.

   You have created a new group. Grouping drawing elements out of existing groups is called nesting. In AutoSketch, you can create up to eight nesting groups.

✔✔✔✔✔ Exercise 6

AutoSketch®
Reference
Manual

In this exercise, create three nested groups shown in the drawing below. First, draw the base of the boat and select the shape for a group. Then add the sail and select it as the second group of drawing elements. Draw the rudder and make its elements a group. Finally, select the entire boat to create a nest of the three previously grouped sets of elements.

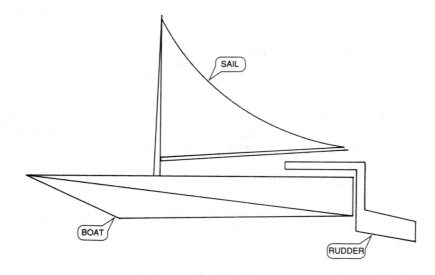

The Ungroup Command

Sometimes you may want to edit only one drawing element in a group. Then you can use the Ungroup command by selecting it from the Change menu. You can use the Alternate key and the F10 key to make selection easier.

p. 210

Selecting one object in a group (either by picking it or by using a crosses or window box) unfastens all the grouped elements. But if the element you want to change is part of a nested group, you must repeat the Ungroup command.

✔✔ Exercise 7

Draw a castle like the one below. Group the left tower and then nest the whole castle. Then ungroup all the elements so that you can erase the left tower.

AutoSketch®
Reference
Manual

pp. 117 -
118

The Move Command

As you draw different shapes on your drawing screen, you may want to relocate some of them to another part of the screen. You could erase objects and then redraw them in new locations. The faster and more efficient method is to use the Move command. With the Move command, you can draw an object and move it where you need it on a drawing. The drawing below shows a car you will draw next and the position you will move it to.

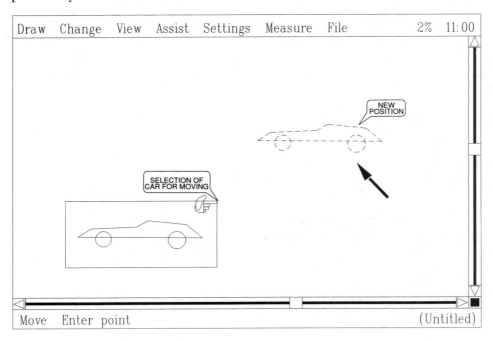

To practice this command, follow these steps:

1. Draw the car.
2. Select the **Move** command.

▶ *Hint:*

You can use the F5 key to select the move command.

3. Select the drawing elements or group you want to move.

▶ *Hint:*

Either the hand pointer or a crosses/window box can indicate your choices.

The prompt "Move From point:" will be displayed. The hand pointer should change to an arrow pointer.

4. Pick a starting point for moving that is either on the objects or close to them.

    As you move your arrow pointer, it will show you where you are moving this base point. As you move the pointer, the elements are dragged into position.

5. Select a point to which the elements should be moved.

✓✓✓ *Exercise 8*

Make a drawing like the one below. Then move the screwdriver to fit into the slot of the bolt head.

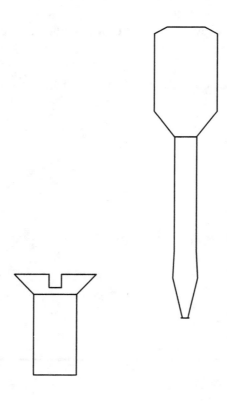

The Copy Command

Think of the Copy command as a Move command that allows you to keep both the original drawing elements and a newly located duplicate of them. With the Copy command, you have great drawing power at your disposal. You can draw one shape and copy it throughout your drawing. If you draw one flower petal, you can use the Copy command to combine copied petals to make a complete flower.

*AutoSketch®
Reference
Manual*
pp. 49 - 50

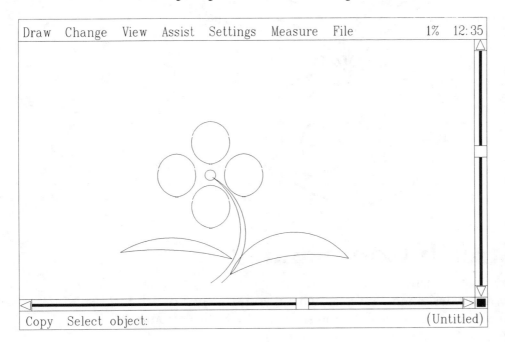

Here's how the command works:

1. Draw a flower petal using the **Arc** command.
2. Select the **Copy** command.

▶ *Hint:*

Pressing the F6 key also activates the Copy command.

3. Select the petal to copy by using a window box.
    The prompt will say "Copy From point:".
4. Select the starting point.
    You will "attach" the copy to your drawing at this base point.
5. Select a point in the drawing where you want the copy to be placed.
6. Copy the petal two more times.
7. Add details to finish the flower.
8. Save the drawing as **Flower**.

✔✔✔✔✔✔ *Exercise 9*

AutoSketch®
Reference
Manual

Create the fruit in the drawing below, and copy it two more times.

The Stretch Command

The Stretch command helps you develop "what if?" situations. For example, if you are designing a race car, what if you stretched out the shape to make a long car, or pushed it in so that it looks like a compact car? The drawing below shows both possibilities.

pp. 187 - 190

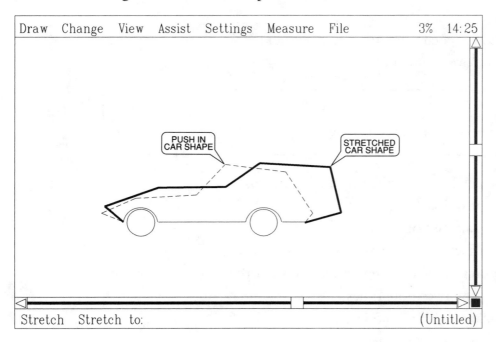

To get an idea of the power of this command, try the following:

1. Draw the box car shown in the drawing below.

    Using the Ortho and Copy commands would speed up the process.

2. Then select the Stretch command.

► *Hint:*

The F7 key also activates this command.

The prompt will ask you to select the first corner.

3. Place a window box around the car. It should not include the baseline of the car or the wheels.

    Always leave part of the object you want to stretch outside of the window box. The part left out will stay in place, and the part selected in the box will move. If the entire object is within the box, the object will move as if you had used the Move command.

    The wheels should not be included because they might also move. If a window box includes the center of a circle, it will move. If not, the circle will stay as it is.

► *Hint:*

If you want to stretch objects in a group, you must select them with a crosses or window box. You can't select them individually. For the Stretch command, both the window and crosses boxes appear dotted because in both cases the window selects everything.

The prompt "Stretch Stretch base:" will be displayed.

4. Now select a point to the left of the left wheel.

This point is the base location. It shows where the stretching will begin.

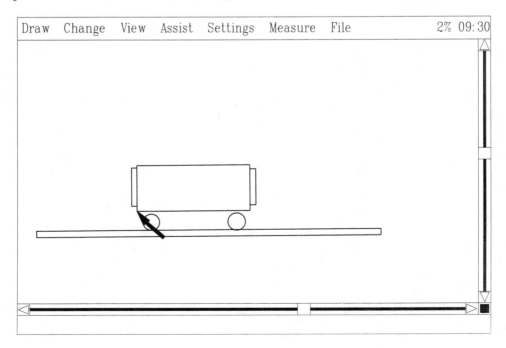

Draw	Change	View	Assist	Settings	Measure	File		2% 09:30

5. Move your arrow pointer to a new position in the drawing area and select it.
What happens to the box car?

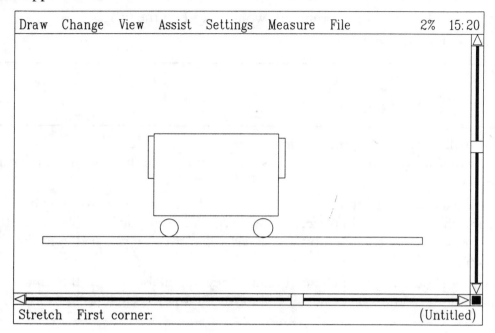

The Scale Command

AutoSketch®
Reference
Manual
pp. 177 -
178

The Scale command is designed to increase or decrease the size of a drawing or drawing parts. This command allows you to draw an object in a convenient size. Then you can enlarge it or shrink it by using the Scale command.

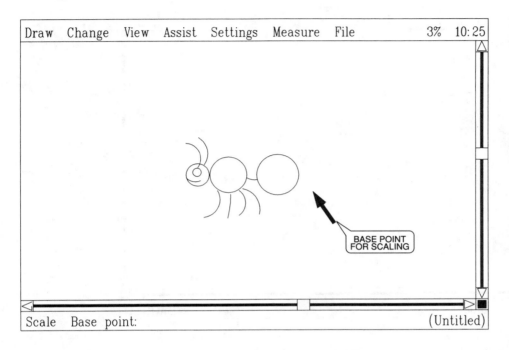

1. Draw an ant like the one in the illustration above.
2. Select the **Scale** command.
3. Then select the ant for enlargement using a crosses or window box.
4. Next, pick a base point as indicated above.

   AutoSketch will scale the object around this point.
5. Now move your pointer to see the object change in size.

   You will see a line from your base point to your arrow pointer location. You can also see the scale factor on the prompt line.
6. When the ant looks something like a prehistoric monster, select that location.

   AutoSketch will redraw the object to be the size you chose.
7. Now shrink the figure to one-half its original size.

The Rotate Command

The Rotate command gives you the ability to turn or revolve a drawing element around any center position. You can spin an object or line it up with other drawing elements.

*AutoSketch®
User
Guide*
**pp. 174 -
176**

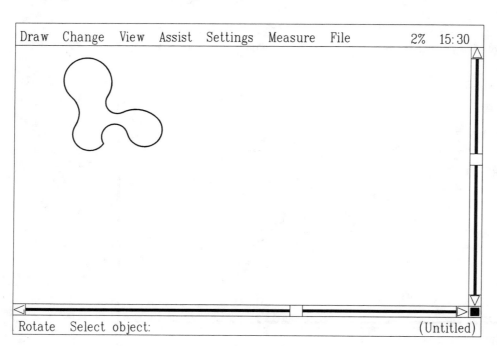

Here's how it works.

1. Draw the figure shown above. Draw it in the location shown so that you will have room to rotate it.

2. Select the Rotate command.

   AutoSketch will prompt you to select objects to rotate.

3. Select the shape with a crosses or window box.

4. Next, pick a point close to the one shown as a center location around which the shape should be rotated.

   Notice that you can drag the element around the center position by moving your pointer.

AutoSketch®
Reference
Manual

5. When the object is in the position shown below, select that location for the second point.

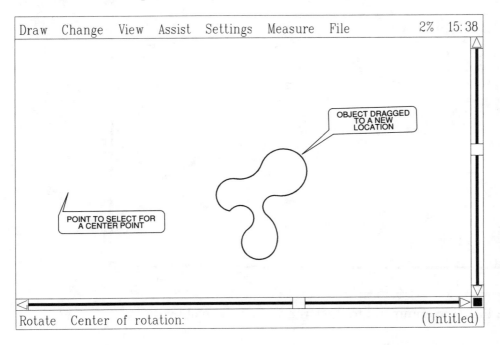

AutoSketch will redraw the shape.

Suppose you wanted to rotate an element at a specific angle. Notice that at the right lower corner of the screen the angle of rotation is displayed.

6. Rotate the object again, this time 90°.

▶ *Hint:*

When you drag the object, you will see a line on the screen as you move your pointer away from the center location. The angle formed by that line and the X-axis in the drawing is the angle of rotation. If that line is exactly horizontal, the angle of rotation is either 0° or 180°, depending on the direction of the line (right or left).

The Mirror Command

pp. 115 - 117

The Mirror command produces a mirror image of something you have drawn. Shapes that are *mirror images* of each other have symmetry; this means that the shape on the left or the top is duplicated by the shape on the right or the bottom. Sometimes such shapes are said to be symmetrical about an axis. Examples of mirror images are the reflection of a landscape on a smooth lake and your likeness reflected in a three-sided mirror.

If you want to draw the same shape more than once or repeat a shape in reverse position, the Mirror command is ideal to use. If an object has symmetry, you need to draw only one half of the object and mirror the rest.

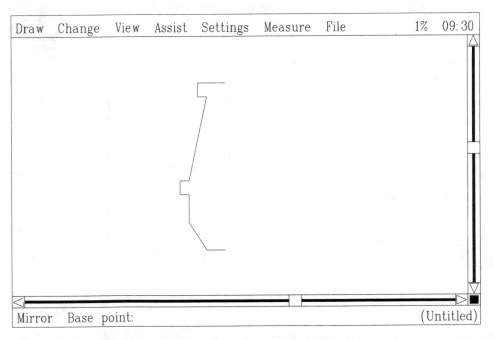

1.   Use the **Polyline** command to draw the shape shown above.

2.   Select the **Mirror** command.

AutoSketch will prompt you to select the elements you want mirrored.

3.   Select the shape.

4.   Then select a base point of the mirror line as shown below.

This line shows the location where you want to draw the reverse image.

▶ *Hint:*

> To create a straight horizontal or vertical mirror line, use the
> Ortho command on the Assist menu.

pp. 119 -
122

5.   Move your pointing device in the direction you want the mirror
     line to run.

6.   When you have dragged the mirror image into place, add it to the
     drawing by selecting the location.

This point is the endpoint of the mirror line. Your drawing should look like the one shown here.

```
Draw   Change   View   Assist   Settings   Measure   File        1%   09:40
```

BASE POINT SELECTED
FOR MIRROR

```
Mirror   Select object:                                          (Untitled)
```

The Property Command

You can use the Property command to change the way an object is displayed on the screen or plotted on paper. You can change any or all of nine properties (qualities):

pp. 164 - 165

- Color
- Line Type
- Dimension Arrow

- Layer
- Font
- Pattern

- Text
- Dimension Units
- Polyline Width

Before you can change these properties, you must set them up with options on the Settings menu. Then use the Change Menu and the Property command to put the changes into effect.

Color and Line Type

Color is one property of a drawing. Different colors are often used in a single drawing to show different objects. You may often choose to show the text for a drawing in a different color than the one used for other elements. The colors you see on your screen depend on the type of monitor you have. Even if your monitor doesn't display colors, you can assign colors to drawing elements that will correspond to ink colors used for plotting the drawing.

pp. 41 - 43

1. Select the **File** menu and the **Open** command to pull out the drawing you saved as FLOWER.

2. Select the **Settings** menu and the **Color** command.

A dialogue box with color selections will be displayed like the one on the next page.

Every time you begin a new drawing, the color is set to black unless you change the color using this option. The check mark shows which color is currently selected.

3. Change the color used to **Red** by picking the box.

AutoSketch®
Reference
Manual
pp. 80 - 86

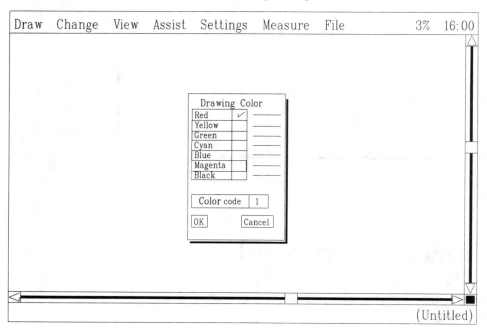

| Draw | Change | View | Assist | Settings | Measure | File | 3% | 16:00 |

Drawing Color

Red	✓	———
Yellow		———
Green		———
Cyan		———
Blue		———
Magenta		———
Black		

Color code | 1

OK   Cancel

(Untitled)

▶ *Hint:*

You could enter a number in the Color Code box to select a color. Codes are 1-7 and are assigned in the order the colors are listed in the box.

A check mark will appear beside the color you selected.

4. Close the dialogue box.

Another property of AutoSketch drawing elements is *line type*. Line type is a combination of line segments and spaces used to distinguish different items in drawings. Examples of line types are dotted lines and dashed lines.

**pp. 108 -
109**

5. Select the **Settings** menu and the **Line Type** command.

A new dialogue box will be displayed with choices of line types. The standard (default) line type is solid. AutoSketch uses this type to draw unless you select a different one.

6. Change the line type to **Dashed**.

Again, the check mark indicates the current line type. Note that the scale factor is .5. You will learn about the scale factor in Unit 10.

7. Close the dialogue box.

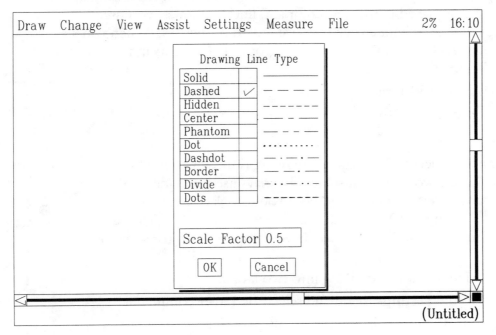

Let's apply these changes to objects in a drawing. First, you must use the Property command from the Settings menu to tell AutoSketch which properties you want to change.

1. Select the **Property** command from the **Settings** menu.

You will see a Change Property Modes dialogue box. AutoSketch will change all properties unless you "turn off" one of the changes by toggling. You want to change the color and line type only.

2. Toggle off all boxes except for **Color** and **Line Type**.

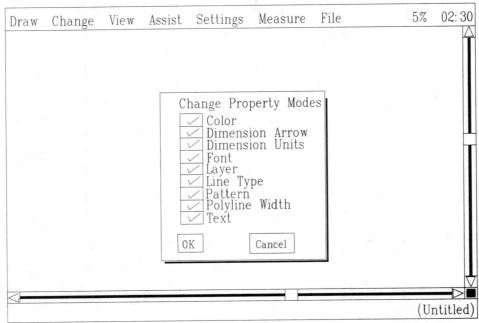

AutoSketch®
Reference
Manual

3. Close the dialogue box.

4. Now select the **Change** menu and the **Property** command.

5. Follow the prompt and select the petals of the flower.

What happens to the petals? If you added more objects to this drawing, they would be displayed in the new color and line type unless you used the Settings menu to change back to the standard properties. When you change properties for an object that is in a group, all elements in the group are changed.

6. Keep the FLOWER drawing to use in the next section.

Layers

The next property of objects in a drawing is the *layer* on which they are drawn. Layers work like transparent overlays used in traditional drafting to group related items together. You can place elements of a drawing on as many as 10 different layers using AutoSketch. You can plot a drawing using all the layers you have set up for it or just some of them.

pp. 102 -
105

Now divide the flower drawing into two layers.

1. Return to the **Settings** menu and select the **Layer** command.

You will see a dialogue box listing the numbers of layers currently activated for the drawing. AutoSketch uses the layer status shown below as the standard. Whenever you begin a new drawing, AutoSketch places all the elements on layer 1. Also, all layers are visible unless you make a change using this dialogue box. This means that when you view a drawing on the screen or plot it on paper all the layers will appear, unless you make the layers invisible.

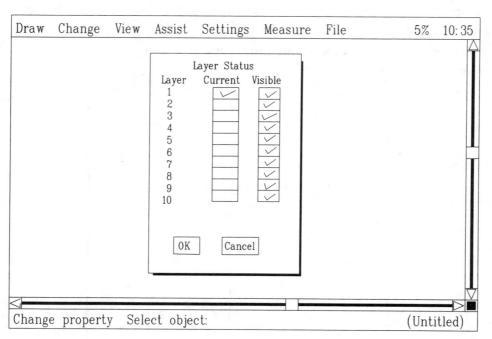

To start drawing objects on a different layer, to return to a finished drawing and move objects to another layer, or to make layers invisible, use the Layer Status dialogue box.

2. Activate layer 3 by picking the box.

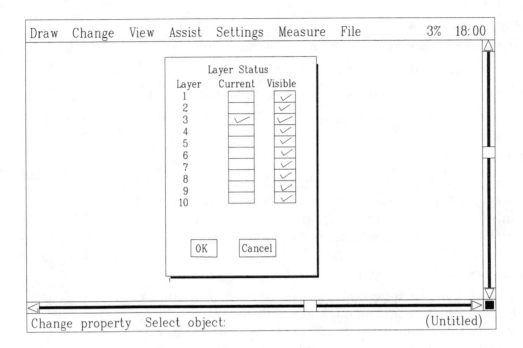

Notice that the check mark moves to this box.

3. Also make layer 3 invisible by toggling off the visible feature.

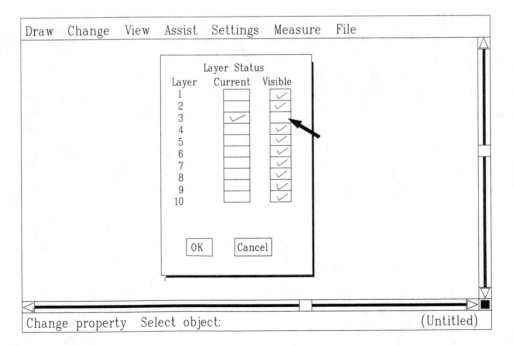

With layer 3 "turned off," objects on it will not appear on the screen or on a paper copy of the drawing.

4.   Close the dialogue box.

5.   Go back to the **Settings** menu to select the **Property** command.

6.   Toggle on **Layer.**

7.   Close the dialogue box.

8.   Select the **Change** menu and the **Property** command.

9.   Last, select the leaves or stem of the flower.

You have transferred the items selected to layer 3. What happens to these objects?

Font and Text

Font is another property that can be changed. You select a new font and apply it with the Property command. A font is a style of text (letters, numbers, symbols, and so on.) The Text option is another way to change the appearance of the text. This option includes such things as height, width, and angle of the text. These choices appear in a dialogue box when you choose the Text command on the Settings menu.

The same dialogue box appears when you use the Settings option of the Text Editor in the Change menu. You will learn how to select new fonts and text options in the section "Text Editor" near the end of this unit. The different fonts you may choose from are shown in that section.

Other Properties

The remaining properties that can be changed with the Change menu are Polyline Width, Pattern Fill, Dimension Units, and Dimension Arrow. These properties must first be set up in the Settings menu. The new properties are then applied with the Property command in the Change menu. You will learn how to make these changes in Unit 10 and 11.

AutoSketch®
Reference
Manual

pp. 192 -
208

The Chamfer Command

AutoSketch®
Reference
Manual
pp. 32 - 37

The Chamfer command places a beveled edge on an entity in your drawing. This command creates a chamfer by trimming two intersecting lines and creating a new line segment. AutoSketch refers to the intersecting lines as objects. You can chamfer entities created with Line, Box, Polyline, or Pattern Fill.

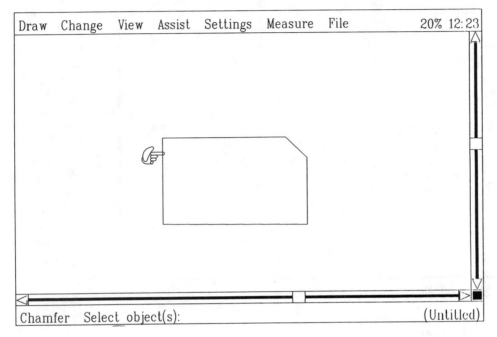

Use the Chamfer command to construct an object similar to the one above.

1. Draw a rectangle using the **Line, Box, Polyline, or Pattern Fill** command.

2. Select the **Chamfer** command.

3. Choose a corner to put the chamfer on.

4. Select one of the corner lines.

5. Select the second corner line.

If both of the lines used to create a chamfer have the same properties, the new line segment will also be the same. For example, if both lines are the same color or line type, the chamfer will have the same color and line type as the original lines. If the lines do not have the same properties, the new lines segment will have the properties currently selected.

The size of the chamfer and the angle are created by selecting sizes from a Settings menu dialogue box. The last line you select tells AutoSketch the location of the Chamfer angle. You will learn how to change these settings in Unit 10.

The Fillet Command

The Fillet command is like the Chamfer command because it completes the corner or intersection of an object by connecting the corner lines with a smooth arc.

Follow the steps to complete the drawing below.

AutoSketch® Reference Manual pp. 88 - 93

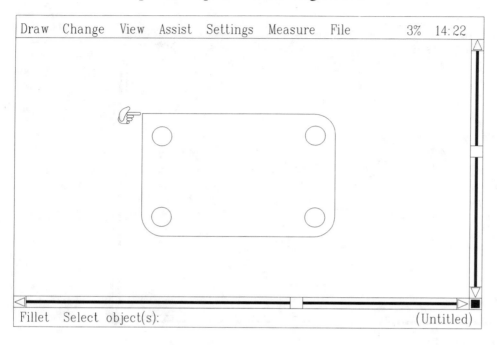

| Draw | Change | View | Assist | Settings | Measure | File | 3% | 14:22 |

Fillet   Select object(s):   (Untitled)

1.   Select the **Fillet** command.
2.   Using the same rectangle you drew for the Chamfer command, select a corner where you want to place a fillet.
3.   Select one of the corner lines.
4.   Select the second corner line.
5.   Add fillets and circles to complete the drawing.

The radius of the fillet is selected from a Settings menu dialogue box. You will learn how to change the radius in Unit 10.

The Box Array Command

The Box Array command is used to make multiple copies of an object in a set pattern. This powerful command creates perfectly straight rows and columns of figures that are exact copies of one original. It displays the real need for CAD in the drawing process because a business profits from the time saved.

1. Draw the object below.

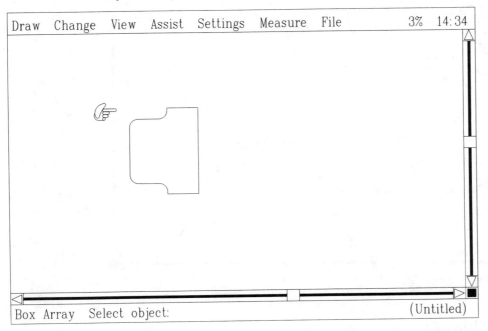

| Draw | Change | View | Assist | Settings | Measure | File | | 3% | 14:34 |

Box Array   Select object: (Untitled)

2. Select the **Box Array** command.

3. Select the object you just made.

Use a crosses/window box, if necessary, to select the entire drawing.

4. Pick a point for the column spacing somewhere near the original object.

The object becomes highlighted once you make that selection.

5. Move the highlighted object to the location you want.

6. Pick a point.

The next prompt is for row spacing, and you choose a point in the same way as the column spacing.

7. Enter a point for the row spacing somewhere near the original object.

8. Move the highlighted object to the location you want.

9. Pick a point.

AutoSketch constructs the array. A dialogue box appears giving you two choices. You may accept or modify the drawing.

10. Select the **Accept** box.

The Ring Array Command

AutoSketch®
Reference
Manual
pp. 169 -
174

The Ring Array command is like the Box Array command because it creates many copies of an object. The difference is that, instead of rows and columns, this command creates a circular pattern.

1.   Draw an object like the one below.

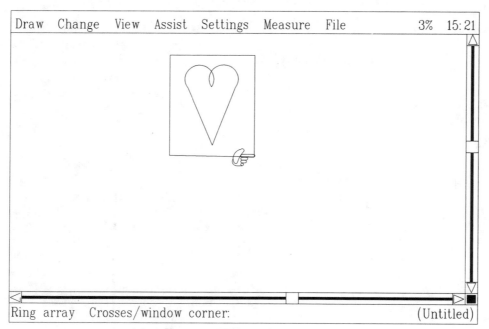

2.   Select the **Ring Array** command.

3.   Select the object.

4.   Select a center point for the new array.

Since the array will be circular, pick a point that provides room to stay on the screen. If the array still goes off, use the Zoom Full command to bring it back.

5.   Choose the **Accept** box.

Text Editor

pp. 194 -
209

The Text Editor in the Change menu is used to change text that already exists on the drawing. The text may have been added with the Quick Text or Text Editor command from the Draw Menu. Each time one or more lines of text are added with the Text Editor in the Draw Menu, the line or lines are treated as one unit. When you want to make a change, they are still treated as one unit. When you select one line of text that was created in the Draw menu, more than one line of text may possibly be selected.

1.   Use the **Text Editor** on the **Draw** menu to create a few lines of text.

2.   Select the **Text Editor** from the **Change** menu.

3. Select the text you created.

A dialogue box appears, with the selected text inside. The box also has scroll bars that allow you to move the text left, right, up, or down. Use the scroll bars to read long lines of text or to read lines of text that do not fit in the window.

Also part of the dialogue box are ten selection blocks to be used while changing text.

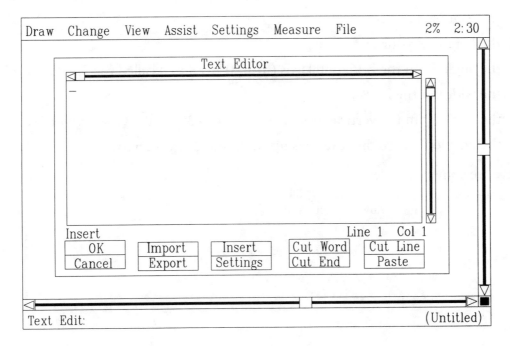

| Draw | Change | View | Assist | Settings | Measure | File | | 2% | 2:30 |

Text Editor

Insert
Line 1 Col 1

| OK | Import | Insert | Cut Word | Cut Line |
| Cancel | Export | Settings | Cut End | Paste |

Text Edit:
(Untitled)

Inserting Text

Insert determines how the new text will be added. New text can overwrite (replace) existing text or be placed within it.

1. Select the **Insert** box.

A highlighted cursor appears. In the lower left corner below the text window, the word "Typeover" also appears. Any new text added will replace the existing text, beginning where the cursor is placed.

2. Pick an insertion point.

3. Type in a new word or sentence.

4. Select **Insert** again.

The highlighted cursor is replaced with an underline cursor. The word "typeover" is replaced by the word "Insert." Text will now be inserted within the existing text.

5. Pick a point and add new text.

6. Select the **OK** box and note the changes in the drawing file.

The Settings Option for Changing Text

The Settings option lets you change the text style or font of text currently contained in the Text Editor box. When you first add text from the Draw menu, AutoSketch uses certain default settings. The default settings create text that is .3" tall, lines up horizontally, has a width factor of 1, and is straight up and down. You can change:

- the font (style)

- the height of your text

- the angle from the horizontal axis (from 0° to 360°) called the *baseline angle*

- the width of the letters

- the angle from the vertical axis (from -30° to +30°) called the *obliquing angle*

- the position where the text lines up (left, right, or centered).

Here are some examples.

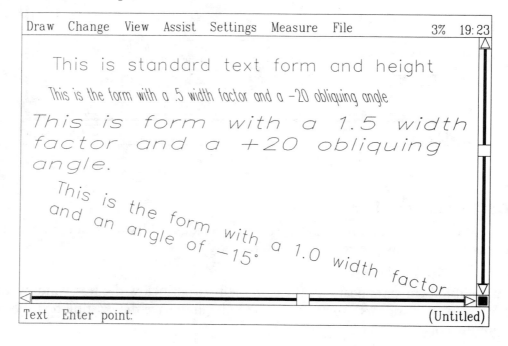

When you select Settings from the Text Editor box, another dialogue box appears (Text and Font Modes).

1. Select the **Text Editor** command on the **Change** menu.

2. Select the text created in the last section.

3. Select the **Settings** box.

This box shows icons (pictures) of different styles of text fonts that you may choose from. If you select the Name box, the fonts will be listed by name only.

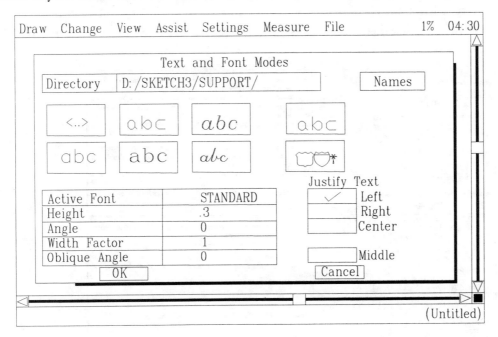

4. Select a Font box.

This makes the font active.

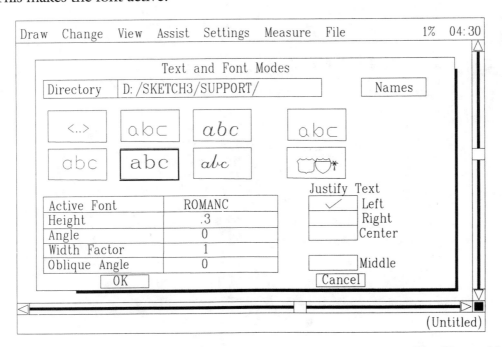

5. Enter the following new values:

    .5 for Height   **.5** for Width factor
    30 for Angle   **20** for the Obliquing angle

6. Select the **Center** box under **Justify Text**.

7. Select **OK** to close the dialogue box.

8. Close the Text Editor dialogue box.

How does the text look now? Notice that it is centered around the insertion point.
The chart below shows the fonts (except Monotxt) that you can choose from.

Name of Font	Examples	Uses
Standard	ABCDEFGHIJKLMNOPQRSTUVWXYZ abcdefghijklmnopqrstuvwxyz 1234567890-=!@#$%^&*()	Lettering. This font is good for general use because it can be drawn quickly and is easy to read.
Romans	ABCDEFGHIJKLMNOPQRSTUVWXYZ abcdefghijklmnopqrstuvwxyz 1234567890-=!@#$%~&*()~	Lettering. The s stands for "simplex." This is a single-stroke, sans-serif font. (Serifs are short lines at the ends of letters. *Sans Serif* means "without serifs.")
Romanc	ABCDEFGHIJKLMNOPQRSTUVWXYZ abcdefghijklmnopqrstuvwxyz 1234567890-=!@#$%~&*()_+~	Lettering. The c stands for "complex." This is a double stroke font, so it is bolder than Romans or Standard. Note that it has serifs
Scriptc	ABCDEFGHIJKLMNOPQRSTUVWXYZ abcdefghijklmnopqrstuvwxyz 1234567890-=!@#$%~&*()_+~	Lettering. This double-stroke font looks like handwriting
Italicc	ABCDEFGHIJKLMNOPQRSTUVWXYZ abcdefghijklmnopqrstuvwxyz 1234567890-=!@#$%~&*()_+~	Lettering. This is a double-stroke font with serifs. Note the slant of the letters.
Symap	[map symbols] 1234567890-=!@#$%~&*()_+~	Mapping. This font contains common symbols used on maps
Symath	[math symbols] 1234567890-=!@#$%~&*()_+~	Mathematics. This font contains math symbols.
Symusic	[music symbols]	Music notation. This symbol is used for writing music.

Key Terms

group   nesting
mirror images   line type
layer

Let's Review

 *Questions*

1. Can you use the Break command to create arcs from circles? Explain.

    _____

    _____

2. What is the difference between the Erase command and the Undo command?

    _____

    _____

3. How does the Redo command work?

    _____

    _____

    _____

4. Explain how drawing elements can be grouped and ungrouped.

    _____

    _____

    _____

5. How would the Move command help speed up the drawing process?

    _____

    _____

6. Give an example of how you would use the Copy command to make a drawing.

    _____

    _____

    _____

7. If you were designing a race car, how could the Stretch command assist you in changing the shape of your car?

_____

_____

_____

8. Explain why the Scale command is useful in drawing.

_____

_____

9. How would you rotate a drawing element at an angle of 60° ?

_____

_____

10. Explain how the Mirror command can help save time in the production of a drawing with symmetrical parts.

_____

_____

11. List the properties of a drawing that can be changed using the Change menu.

_____

_____

_____

12. How does the Text Editor command in the Change menu differ from the Text Editor command in the Draw menu?

_____

_____

13. Name three ways you can change the appearance of text in a drawing.

_____

_____

_____

Problems

1. Make a drawing of the floor plan of your bedroom. Use the mirror command to produce two bedrooms. Then produce four bedrooms.

2. Use the drawing you created in the first problem. To one bedroom only, add a picture of your bed and a chest of drawers. Then make each piece of furniture a different color.

3. Using the drawing for problem 2, copy the bed and chest of drawers into the other bedrooms you created in problem 1.

Extend Your Knowledge

1. Sketch half of a heart. Now place a mirror edge by the object, and reflect the image to see a whole heart. Which command is this activity like?

2. Ask a photographer how she or he uses photographic equipment to copy, scale, rotate, and stretch images. Compare these processes to the operation of the Change command.

3. Use an overhead projector to experiment with rotating and scaling. Turn the projector on, place a pencil on it, and draw the expanded object. Make a drawing after each of the following:

   ■ rotate the pencil

   ■ scale by moving the focuser up

   ■ scale by moving the focuser down.

AutoSketch on Trial

by Tyrrell Armstrong

April 23, 1987—Friday afternoon. It was 5:00 p.m. and I was just leaving the Palm Bay police station where I work as director of information management services. Several miles away about the same time, William Cruse was pulling out of his driveway.

Armed with a shotgun, a revolver, and a semi-automatic rifle, Cruse drove through his neighborhood. He fired several shotgun blasts at people across the street from his own residence. Cruse then drove into a shopping center and started firing his rifle, killing three people. Several police units arrived just as Cruse was leaving the scene in his car. The police chased him across the street to another shopping center, where Cruse jumped from his vehicle carrying his weapons. Within six minutes, Cruse had killed a total of six people, including two police officers.

For the next ten hours, police from many agencies surrounded the area and negotiated with Cruse, who had taken several hostages. Eventually, the negotiating team managed to have the hostages released, and the police smoked the murderer out of the building. Cruse surrendered, unscathed. The ordeal was over.

After the fact, much evidence was gathered, but there were some scenarios that needed to be reconstructed. There were more than 100 witnesses that could be called to the stand. Detailed documentation was very important, and it had to be provided immediately. I decided to build a map of the shopping centers. Witnesses would then review the map and place themselves within it according to their sworn testimony.

AutoCAD, I knew, would do the job nicely, but I did not have time to learn it sufficiently before the impending interview date. However, I did learn AutoSketch. The only other graphic tool I had on hand was CompuBrush by Rix.

Armed with blueprints of the two shopping centers and the first version of AutoSketch, I sat down in a locked room and 12 hours later, I had the desired map. As a witness sat next to me, I panned and zoomed across the entire scene, finally settling in on that portion of the stage where he or she was personally involved.

In the years since William Cruse was arrested, I've continued to apply AutoSketch to my work almost daily. Did CAD help build the case against William Cruse? I think it did, but only the jurors could say for sure. On April 5th, 1989, seven women and five men found William Cruse guilty of six counts of first-degree murder, and associated charges of abduction and attempted murder.

Excerpted from CADENCE, September 1989, Copyright © 1989, Ariel Communications, Inc.

Illustration: Tyrrell Armstrong, Courtesy of Ariel Communications, Inc.

UNIT 8

The View Menu

Objectives:
- *To produce different views of a drawing.*
- *To understand how to remove unwanted marks from a drawing.*

AutoSketch®
Reference
Manual

pp. 214-
215

The commands on the View menu are designed to let you change your viewpoint in looking at a drawing. You can zoom in on some part of a drawing, move far away to view the drawing from a distance, or get a view of a drawing from a point to the left or right of the drawing (instead of center).

| Draw | Change | View | Assist | Settings | Measure | File | 24% | 12:21 |

Last Plot Box
Last View   F9

Zoom X   F10
Zoom Full
Zoom Limits
Zoom X

Pan   F8

Redraw

(Untitled)

These commands shift your point of view without changing the original drawing. AutoSketch always stores the coordinates of the points you selected when you made the drawing. The View commands change the location of the drawing display on the screen.

The Zoom X Command

The powerful Zoom X command allows you to magnify (enlarge) or reduce a drawing. You can make a drawing a specific size or just a size that is easy to work with.

To use the Zoom X command, you indicate in a dialogue box a *scale* or zoom *factor* that you want AutoSketch to use when making the drawing bigger or smaller. Entering a zoom factor of less than 1 (for example, .5) shrinks the display of the drawing. A zoom factor larger than 1 (for example, 2) enlarges the drawing to show greater detail on the screen.

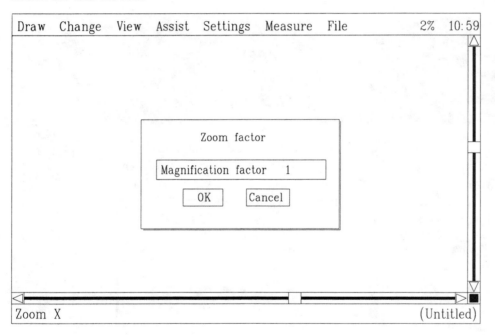

Let's see how the command works.

1. Load AutoSketch.
2. Make a drawing like the one below.
3. Select the **Zoom X** command.

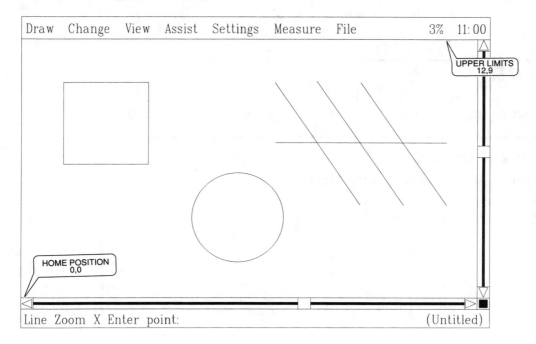

```
Draw   Change   View   Assist   Settings   Measure   File        3%   11:00
```
UPPER LIMITS
12,9

HOME POSITION
0,0

```
Line Zoom X Enter point:                                        (Untitled)
```

A dialogue box for entering a zoom factor will be displayed. Notice that AutoSketch reminds you what Draw command you were using before you zoomed by displaying it in the prompt area along with the Zoom prompt.

4. Highlight the empty box to the right of the **Magnification Factor** box and type 2.
5. Close the dialogue box.

What happens to the drawing?

▶ *Hint:*

Remember that whatever is in the center of the drawing at its original size remains in the center of the screen area when you zoom in or out. Knowing this should help you keep track of what you are looking at when most of your drawing is off the screen area.

6. Now use **Zoom X** again, and change the zoom factor to .25.

The drawing should be half its original size.

The Zoom Box Command

Another way to zoom in on a drawing is by using the Zoom Box command. With this command, you select two points for corners of a box. This box shows the part of the drawing that AutoSketch will enlarge or reduce. Whatever is inside the Zoom box will be enlarged to fill the screen area.

*AutoSketch®
Reference
Manual*
**pp. 217-
218**

▶ ## *Hint:*

Unlike a crosses or window box, the zoom box can be stretched either to the right or the left of the first corner you enter for it.

Let's use this command.

1. Select the **File** menu and the **Open** command.

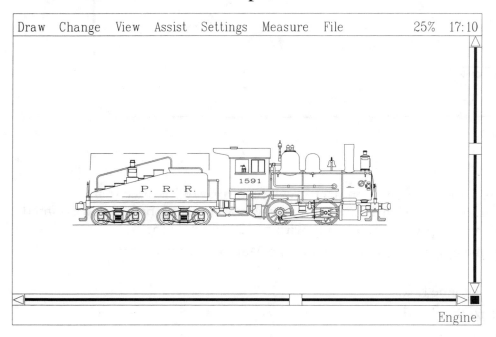

2. Bring up the **ENGINE** drawing.

3. Select the **Zoom box** command.

4. Select corners so that the zoom box contains only one section of the drawing, as shown below.

AutoSketch®
Reference
Manual

► *Hint:*

If you press the F10 key, you won't need to pull down the View menu.

The elements contained in the zoom box should enlarge to fill the screen area. You should be able to see much more detail.

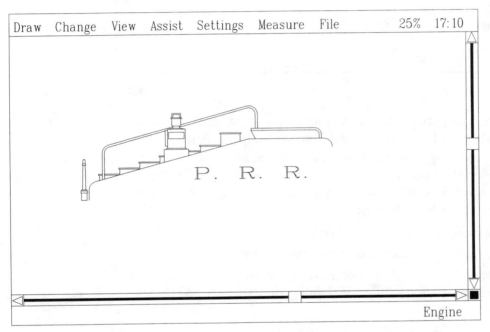

5. Now zoom in again on the corner you just selected. Even more detail will be visible.

The Zoom Limits Command

pp. 218 - 219

When you use the Zoom Limits command, AutoSketch redraws to fill the screen area with any objects or empty space within the drawing limits. The drawing limits, or the available area for a drawing, are set up with coordinate values that you can change. AutoSketch starts with the point 0,0 (called *home position*) for the bottom left corner of the drawing and the point 12,9 for the top right corner.

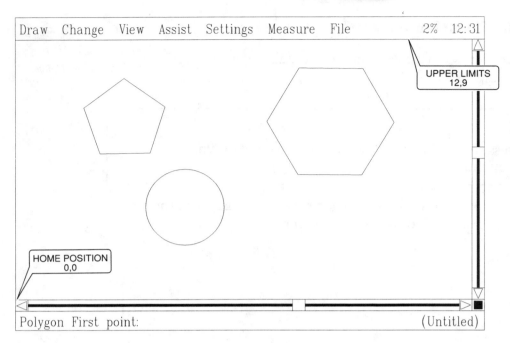

Your screen display is like the whole sheet of paper you use in traditional drafting. The units used for coordinates in AutoSketch can represent anything you want, such as inches, miles, or millimetres. For example, let's say you decide on inches for the unit. Your screen would be similar to the standard size of notebook paper which measures 11 x 8 1/2 inches.

1. Make a drawing like the one above.

2. Select the **Settings** menu and the **Limits** command.

You see the drawing limits AutoSketch starts with. If you want the screen to represent a larger sheet of paper, you can change the drawing limits.

3. Change the lower limits (Left, Bottom) to **2,2** and the upper limits (Right, Top) to **24,18**.

4. Close the box.

5. To view the new limits, select the **Zoom Limits** command on the **View** menu.

6. Repeat steps two through five, but use **-2,-2** for the lower limits and **36,24** for the upper limits.

How does the view of the drawing change?

The Zoom Full Command

Sometimes when you use the Zoom limits command the drawing won't fit on the screen area; that is, the drawing is larger than the current drawing limits. You can't display all of it on the screen at the same time at the enlarged size. To correct this situation, all you need to do is use the Zoom Full command.

p. 218

This command fills the entire screen area with all the drawing contained within the *drawing extents*. The drawing extents make up the area of the drawing that includes objects, like a drawing on paper without any empty space around the edges. Depending on the values you have entered using the Limits command, the drawing extents may be the same as the drawing limits or they may be larger.

1. Draw three circles that look like the ones below.

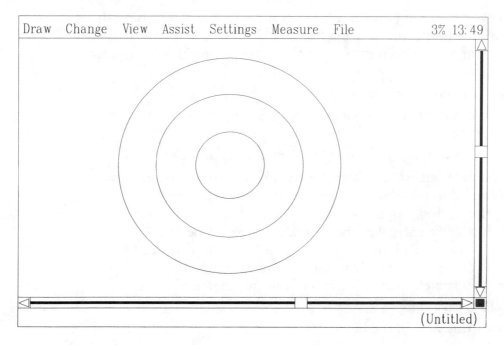

2. Then use Zoom limits to enlarge them until they are too large to be displayed on the screen.

▶ *Hint:*

Decrease the upper limits.

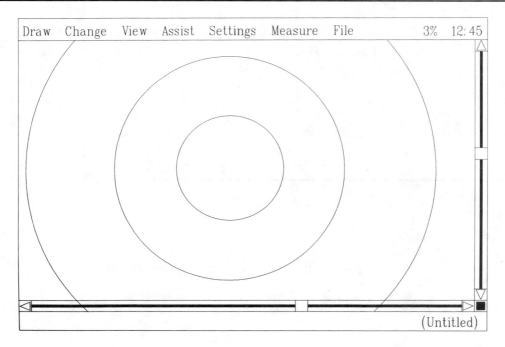

3. Now use the **Zoom full** command to make the circles fit the drawing area.

AutoSketch®
Reference
Manual
pp. 123 -
124

The Pan Command

To *pan* a drawing means to get a complete view of it. Using the Pan command shifts the drawing horizontally to a new location on the screen. AutoSketch prompts you to select two points in order to move the drawing:

- a reference point on the drawing itself
- another point showing where you want the drawing to be placed.

Your drawing will not be changed in the panning process.

A handy feature that makes AutoSketch easy to use is the rubber band attached to the object being moved. (When the drawing is moved, the reference point is attached to the second point by the rubber band.) Just like an actual rubber band, this line can be moved, stretched, crossed, and uncrossed. It is visible until you select the point to which you want the view moved. The new view is determined by the distance you stretch the rubber band from the reference point.

Let's try panning.

1. Draw this view of the house.

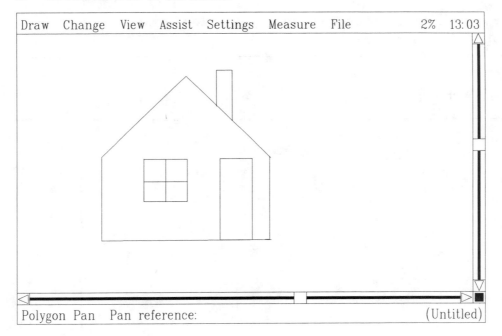

| Draw Change View Assist Settings Measure File | 2% 13:03 |

Polygon Pan   Pan reference: (Untitled)

2. Select the **Pan** command.

The Draw command prompt will still be displayed along with the Pan prompt.

▶ *Hint:*

You can use the F8 key to activate this feature.

3.   Select the lower right corner of the house for a reference point.

4.   Pan the house to the right by stretching the rubber band in that direction.

5.   Select the second point as the pan destination.

AutoSketch will redraw the house in the part of the screen you selected.

▶ *Hint:*

Remember that you can pan an object off the screen, outside the drawing limits, if you need extra space to draw. You can also enter coordinates for the reference point and destination point if you need to locate the drawing more precisely. When you want to pan a drawing straight vertically or horizontally, turn on Ortho.

The Last View Command

The Last View command does just what its name implies. Selecting it returns the last view displayed on the screen. It lets you go back and forth between the current view of a drawing and the previous one.

pp. 101 - 102

1.   Draw a square with a circle inside it.

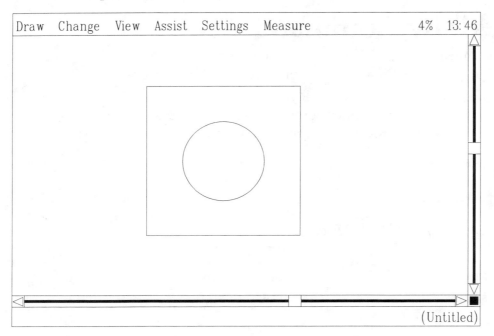

2.   Select the **Zoom X** command.

3.   Change the zoom factor to **.25**.

4.   Use the **Last View** command.

What happens to the drawing?

5.   Select **Zoom X** again, and use **2** as the zoom factor.

6.   Now look at the last view again.

▶ *Hint:*

   Try using the F9 key.

As you have seen, this command lets you flip back and forth between views. If you continue to press the F9 key, the last two drawing views will be displayed alternately again and again.

The Last Plot Box Command

   When you plot a drawing, you can choose which part of the drawing appears on the paper by creating a plot box. The Last Plot Box command fills the screen with the last plot box you created. You will learn to use this command in Unit 12 after you learn to create a plot box.

p. 101

The Redraw Command

   The last command on the View menu is the Redraw command. It is usually used to clean up a drawing after you have edited intersecting objects.

   Another way to select the Redraw command is to pick the black square at the bottom right corner of the drawing screen.

p. 167

 *Key Terms*

scale factor   drawing limits
home position   drawing extents
pan

Let's Review

Questions

1. When you enter a scale factor, which Zoom command are you using? What scale factor could you enter to make a drawing smaller?

   _____

   _____

2. How is making a zoom box different from making a crosses/window box?

   _____

   _____

3. What is the Zoom Limits command used for?

   _____

   _____

4. Are the resulting views produced by using the Zoom Limits command and the Zoom Full command always different? Explain.

   _____

   _____

   _____

5. What happens to a drawing when you use the Pan command?

   _____

   _____

6. Why is the Last View command useful?

   _____

   _____

   _____

7. When do you usually use the Redraw command?

_____

_____

Extend Your Knowledge

1. Find a picture of a new sports car in a magazine. Think of two ways you could double the size of the picture, without using AutoSketch. Then use grid paper to reduce the sports car to half its size. Keep all parts proportional to the car in the picture.

2. Place a pencil on a sheet of grid paper. Trace the shape of the pencil. Then count the number of squares on the grid paper inside the traced shape. Count squares to redraw the pencil three times the original size.

3. Adjust a pair of binoculars to your eyes. Then focus on a window so that you see all of the window from inside a room. Refocus so that you look through the window, outside, at some object a good distance away. What happens to the window frame? Using the Zoom commands is like focusing on an object with a pair of binoculars.

The Assist Menu

AutoSketch®
Reference
Manual

Objective:

■ *To learn about the drawing tools offered by AutoSketch.*

The Assist menu provides tools to make drawing with AutoSketch easier. A handy feature of this menu is that it keeps track of which tools you have activated.

pp. 9 - 10

Draw	Change	View	Assist	Settings	Measure	File		24%	11:30

```
                    Arc Mode   C1
                    Attach     A8
                    Coords
                    Fill
                    Frame
                    Grid       A6
                    Ortho      A5
                    Snap       A7
                    View Icons

                    Record Macro
                    Play Macro
                    User Input C10
```

(Untitled)

If there is a check mark in front of the command on the menu, then you have already given the command to AutoSketch to "turn on" the drawing aid. It is currently in use. If there is no check mark, the tool is "turned off." Each time you open the file to choose a different drawing to edit or make a new drawing, AutoSketch turns off these tools. If you want to use them, you must enter commands.

Which tools are turned on in this Assist menu?

AutoSketch®
Reference
Manual

```
┌──────────────────────────────────────────────────────────────────────┐
│ Draw  Change  View  Assist  Settings  Measure  File      0%    19:47   │
│                    ┌─────────────────┐                            ▲    │
│        .      .    │ Arc Mode  C1    │  .    .    .    .    .      █    │
│                    │ Attach    A8    │                                 │
│                    │✓Coords          │                                 │
│                    │ Fill            │                                 │
│                    │ Frame           │                                 │
│        .      .    │✓Grid      A6    │  .    .    .    .    .           │
│                    │ Ortho     A5    │                                 │
│                    │✓Snap      A7    │                            █    │
│                    │ View Icons      │                                 │
│                    ├─────────────────┤                                 │
│                    │ Record Macro    │                                 │
│                    │ Play Macro      │                                 │
│                    │ User Input C10  │                                 │
│                    └─────────────────┘                                 │
│                                                                        │
│        .      .      +        .    .    .    .    .    .                │
│                    ↖                                                    │
│                                                                        │
│        .      .      .        .    .    .    .    .    .                │
│                                                                        │
│                                                                   ▼    │
│ ◁────────────────────────────█────────────────────────────────▷  ■    │
│                       3.0000,3.0000                    (Untitled)      │
└──────────────────────────────────────────────────────────────────────┘
```

You can turn the drawing aids on at any time while you are using AutoSketch. For example, you could be in the middle of an editing sequence and decide that you need help in measuring. All you would need to do is select the Grid command and continue working. The Grid would be displayed for your use until you turn it off or until you end the AutoSketch session.

The Coords Command

The Coords command turns on or off the coordinates displayed at the bottom of the screen, as shown in the drawing above. They are called running coordinates because they give you the X and Y values of the pointer at all times as it moves around the screen.

pp. 47 - 49

If you use the Coordinates command while you are also using the Scale or Rotate command, the scale factor or rotation angle will be displayed in place of coordinates.

The Coords command can also show polar coordinates in the upper right corner of the screen. For example, if you create a line, the polar coordinates are displayed when you pick the second point.

The Arc Mode Command

The Arc Mode command changes the way the Polyline command works. When the Arc Mode command is off, the Polyline command draws straight, connected lines. When the Arc Mode command is turned on, the Polyline command draws arcs that are connected to each other.

AutoSketch®
Reference
Manual

1. Select the **Assist** menu and turn on the **Arc Mode** command.

2. Select the **Polyline** command from the **Draw** menu.

3. Select three points.

    You can see the arc that will be added to the drawing.

4. Select two more points to create another arc.

    Note that this arc is attached to the first arc.

5. Create a few more arcs.

6. Pick the last point of the arc to finish the series of arcs.

The Ortho Command

If you have been using a pointing device, you already know that it is sometimes hard to draw completely straight lines. The Ortho command helps you draw horizontal and vertical lines that are straight.

pp. 119 - 122

Remember, though, that if you have Ortho turned on, you can't draw diagonal lines or move the rubber band in a diagonal direction. (You can move your pointer diagonally, but the lines will only move horizontally or vertically, no matter how you move your pointer.) You can draw only straight lines using this tool.

How does the Rotate command work when Ortho is turned on? You can still rotate an object, but only to angles that are straight across or straight up and down—0, 90, 180, and 270°.

▶ *Hint:*

To turn on Ortho, press the Alt key and the F5 key.

Exercise 1

Load AutoSketch. Create the drawing below using Ortho.

AutoSketch®
Reference
Manual

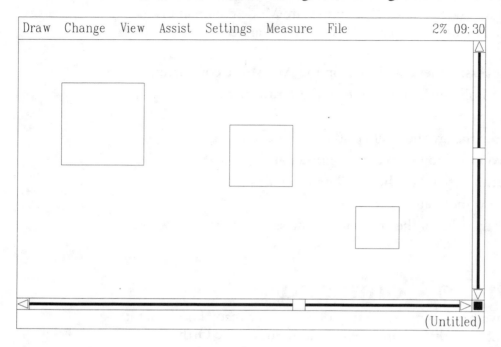

The Grid Command

When you need to measure while you draw, turn on the *grid*. The screen will be filled with a pattern of dots. They can be evenly spaced, making a square pattern (for example, 2 x 2 or 4 x 4) or unevenly spaced, making a rectangular pattern (for example, 2 x 4 or 1 x 3). If you wanted to make a drawing two or three times larger in one direction than in the other, an uneven pattern would be useful. The dots can also be close together or far apart. You can also make your grid smaller than a unit of 1, resulting in more grid points.

You can choose how you want your grid to look by using the Grid command on the Settings menu and entering X and Y values. You will read more about this command in Unit 10. When you turn on the grid, the dots are evenly spaced, 1 unit apart. This kind of grid will be displayed unless you change the settings. The grid will cover the drawing area you have set up by entering the drawing limits.

pp. 96 - 98

▶ Hint:

Use the Alt key and the F6 key to turn on the grid. You can also toggle it on by using the dialogue box for Grid on the Settings menu.

Exercise 2

Use the Grid command to help you create the drawing below.

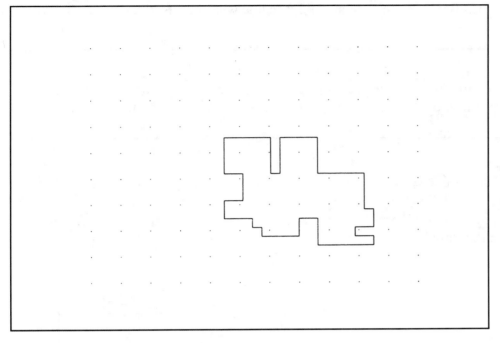

AutoSketch®
Reference
Manual

pp. 185 -
187

The Snap Command

The Snap command is used to help you select an exact point in a drawing. When Snap has been turned on, only points defined by snap spacing can be selected. The result is that you can only move your pointing device to a snap point. If you try to stop between points, AutoSketch will *snap* or jump to the nearest snap point, automatically selecting that point for you. When you turn on Snap, the spacing is set at 1 x 1 (1 unit horizontally, 1 unit vertically). If you want to change the spacing, use the Snap option on the Settings menu. Snap spacing may be different from the spacing of the grid displayed.

Watch for a small cross to follow the movement across the screen when Snap is turned on. This cross will automatically jump to the nearest snap point as you move the pointer. If you pan a drawing, the object will move to the nearest Snap point. With Snap, you can control the distance the object is shifted.

▶ Hint:

If you can't find your snap cross, your snap setting may be too large for the screen. In this case, go to the Settings menu and decrease the distance between snap points.

One of the terms you will come across in CAD is *snap-to-grid*, an easy method of drawing a line to an exact location. For this method, use the same unit values for the Grid and Snap commands. You can find an approximate location using the grid. Then all you need to do is come close to this destination with your pointer when you are selecting a point. Because of the Snap tool, the line will jump to the exact point you need.

▶ *Hint:*

A fast way to turn on Snap is pressing the Alt key and the F7 key. You can also toggle Snap on by using the dialogue box for Snap on the Settings menu.

✔✔✔✔✔ *Exercise 3*

List the approximate X and Y coordinates for making the shape below. Then use Snap to create the drawing.

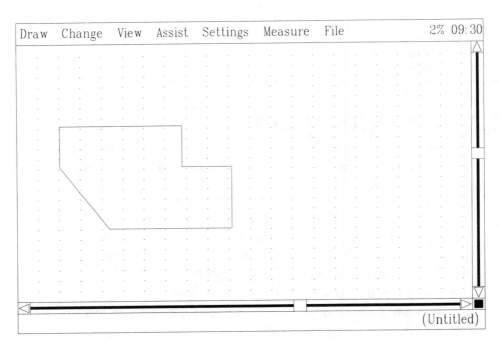

The Attach Command

AutoSketch®
Reference
Manual

pp. 10 - 17

Sometimes when you are making a drawing, you might want to draw an object and then add elements to it at exact locations. For example, if you draw two lines and want to connect a third line, it's easy with the Attach command.

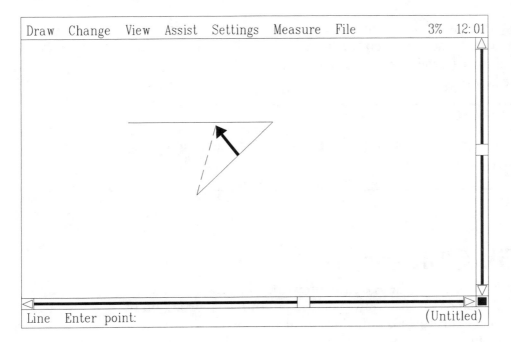

```
Draw   Change   View   Assist   Settings   Measure   File        3%   12:01


Line   Enter point:                                              (Untitled)
```

When you use a Draw command with this tool activated, AutoSketch searches your drawing for an *attach point* for connecting the new object. When it finds an attach point, the object attaches to the point you pick or to the nearest attach point. Sometimes these are the same point; sometimes they are different. The object will attach itself to the nearest attach point on a drawing even if you selected another point.

If you have the Attach tool turned on, AutoSketch can use the following attach modes:

- Center
- End Point
- Intersect
- Midpoint
- Node Point
- Perpendicular
- Quadrant
- Tangent

You will learn about these choices in Unit 10. You can toggle them on and off using the Attach option on the Settings menu.

▶ *Hint:*

To select the Attach feature, press the Alt key and the F8 key, or toggle it on using the Attach dialogue box from the Settings menu.

The Frame Command

AutoSketch®
Reference
Manual
pp. 93 - 95

The Frame command works closely with the Curve command on the Draw menu. The Curve command changes straight lines into a curve through control points. The control points used to draw a curve make up the frame. The more points you use, the better the curve will fit the frame.

To make this frame visible on the screen, turn on this drawing tool with the Frame command. When the frame is turned on, you can select a curve by pointing to the frame. It is hard to select a curve for editing unless Frame is turned on.

▶ *Hint:*

You can also toggle Frame on by using the Curve dialogue box on the Settings menu.

The Fill Command

pp. 87 - 88

The Fill command on the Assist menu works with the Polyline and Pattern Fill commands on the Draw menu. Pattern Fill is turned on by default when you load AutoSketch. This means that when you create an object such as a filled polygon, the pattern appears inside the object. If the Fill command is turned off, the pattern does not appear.

This command changes only the way you see the object on the screen; the object is not actually changed. One way you might want to use this feature is when you choose commands (such as Zoom commands) that cause AutoSketch to redraw the screen. With Pattern Fill off, the screen will redraw much faster.

The View Icons Command

AutoSketch®
Reference
Manual
p. 215

In earlier units, you saw icons that represent Part File drawings, such as in the Part File dialogue box shown here. You also saw icons that represent text fonts. The View Icons command is turned on as the default when you load AutoSketch. If you turn View Icons off, items such as drawings and text fonts will be displayed by name only. You can toggle View Icons on or off from the Assist menu. You can also select the Name box in the upper right corner of the dialogue box.

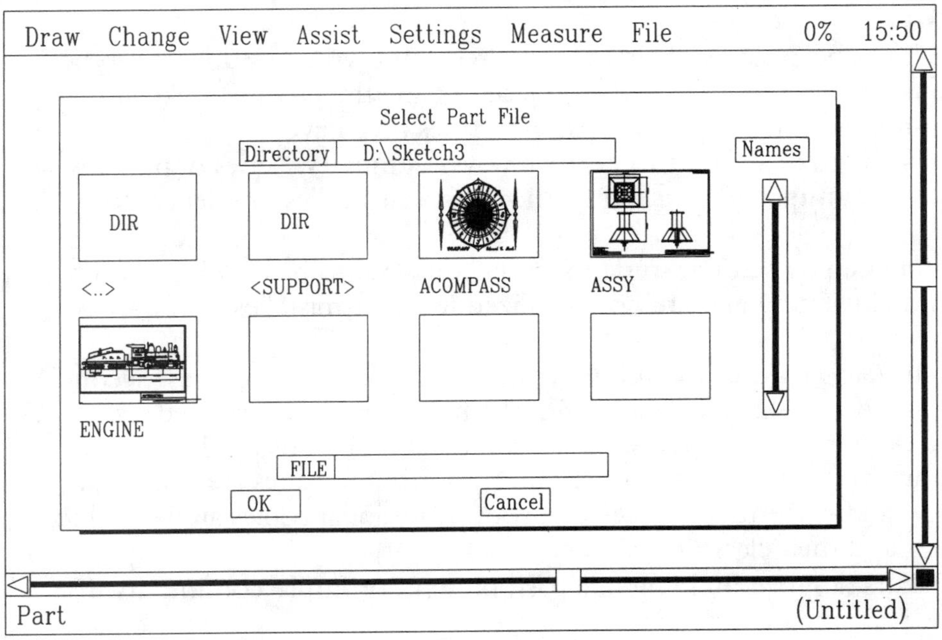

```
Draw   Change   View   Assist   Settings   Measure   File          0%   15:50

                        Select Part File
            Directory  D:\Sketch3                        Names

      ┌──────────┐  ┌──────────┐  ┌──────────┐  ┌──────────┐
      │          │  │          │  │          │  │          │
      │   DIR    │  │   DIR    │  │          │  │          │
      │          │  │          │  │          │  │          │
      └──────────┘  └──────────┘  └──────────┘  └──────────┘
        <..>         <SUPPORT>     ACOMPASS        ASSY

      ┌──────────┐  ┌──────────┐  ┌──────────┐  ┌──────────┐
      │          │  │          │  │          │  │          │
      │          │  │          │  │          │  │          │
      │          │  │          │  │          │  │          │
      └──────────┘  └──────────┘  └──────────┘  └──────────┘
       ENGINE

                    FILE
            OK                      Cancel

Part                                                      (Untitled)
```

The Macro Commands

pp. 109 -
113

There are three commands–Record Macro, User Input, and Play Macro–that you can use to create and run macros. Macros are programs that record a series of actions that you want AutoSketch to perform by itself. You can use it to make a record of things you do over and over. This can save time and eliminate errors in selecting items from AutoSketch menus. The Play macro command will be grayed out if you do not have a macro ready to use.

Key Terms

grid   snap
snap-to-grid   attach point

It's Elementary CAD

by Ken Ford

Sauquoit Valley Central School in upstate New York has approximately 1,450 students (K through 12). Sauquoit Valley's computer program is known throughout the state for its interactive use of computer technology.

From the start, Sauquoit recognized the need for its students to be exposed to computer-aided design and graphics. Elementary students use AutoSketch, word processing, and desktop publishing to compose, illustrate, and publish stories. They are encouraged to select their own topics and write about things they know or care about.

AutoSketch has been a great help for some reluctant writers; students can be encouraged to write captions or narratives to accompany the pictures. Likewise, these young writers are often eager to illustrate stories they have written. Autosketch can be used in a variety of creative ways—a mural, a series of pictures, or a comic book to summarize concepts learned in social studies or science, for example.

In a non-threatening setting, students are encouraged to be creative in both their writing and illustrating and are not penalized for their mistakes. They are encouraged to be risk takers.

AutoSketch is also used in second, fourth, and sixth grade art classes. Second grade students write and illustrate books with the help of program-trained sixth grade students. Because their sentences are short, text commands can be used to print the story and pictures together more quickly. Once the pages are printed, the books are bound and each student receives a copy. Additional copies are bound for the media center and their classroom library.

Fourth graders design a building in a past, present, or future community. If they choose the past, the building has to incorporate details from Greek, Roman, medieval, or colonial American time periods; the present, Frank Lloyd Wright and his concept of designing to fit the environment rather than destroying the environment to fit the building; the future, styles from both past and present.

Sixth grade students are also taught how to use the AutoSketch program. They are allowed to design pictures and discover more on their own about the capabilities of AutoSketch.

Building on the skills acquired at the elementary level, students go on to use AutoCAD in junior high and high school. The illustration shown here is a class exercise of a pipe construction of a student's name, which shows how to utilize the Block command in AutoCAD.

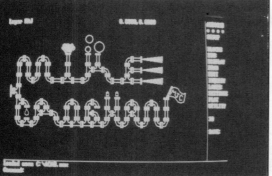

The CAD programs provided at Sauquoit Valley Central School give students the conceptual tools they need in a world of high technology and, in doing so, guarantee a skilled work force in years to come.

Ken Ford is a computer instructor and assistant principal at Sauquoit Valley Central School in upstate New York.

Excerpted from CADENCE, May 1990, Copyright 1990, Ariel Communications, Inc.

Let's Review

Questions

1. How do you know which AutoSketch drawing aids are in use as you draw?

   _____

   _____

2. What is the Ortho command used for?

   _____

3. Can you rotate an object when Ortho is turned on? Explain.

   _____

   _____

   _____

4. The first time you enter the Grid command, what spacing does AutoSketch use for the grid?

   _____

   _____

5. How is the Snap command useful in making a drawing?

   _____

   _____

6. What is an attach point?

   _____

   _____

7. What command on the Draw menu is the Frame command used with?

   _____

   _____

8. What command on the Draw menu is the Arc Mode command used with?

    _____

    _____

9. If you use a Zoom command, which command might speed up the screen redraw?

    _____

    _____

 *Extend Your Knowledge*

1. Use a magnet, a steel finish nail, and a piece of cardboard to illustrate the Attach command. Place the nail on top of the cardboard. Then take the cardboard and hold it above a magnet. Move the magnet under the cardboard close to the nail and watch the nail jump to the point where the magnet is located under the cardboard. CAUTION: To prevent damage to the computer or disks, do this activity somewhere other than the room they are in.

2. Try the following activity to see how the Frame command works in AutoSketch. Draw four freehand boxes all connected end to end to form one large rectangle. Draw half circles on the outer ends of the first and fourth rectangle. Then draw a half circle on the left edge of the second rectangle. You have just drawn a paper clip.

The Settings Menu

AutoSketch®
Reference
Manual

pp.180 -
181

Objectives:
- *To change settings for drawing and editing commands.*
- *To to set up properties of drawings.*
- *To set limits for the drawing area.*

As you make drawings with AutoSketch, you can use the Settings menu to tell AutoSketch how you want some of the Draw, Change, and Measure commands to work.

Draw	Change	View	Assist	Settings	Measure	File

Arrow
Attach
Box Array
Chamfer
Color
Curve
Ellipse
Fillet
Grid
Layer
Limits
Line Type
Part Base
Pattern
Pick
Polyline
Property
Ring Array
Snap
Text
Units

(Untitled)

When you select options on the Settings menu, a dialogue box will be displayed on the screen. You can enter selections in a dialogue box to set up or change the operation of commands from other menus.

AutoSketch®
Reference
Manual

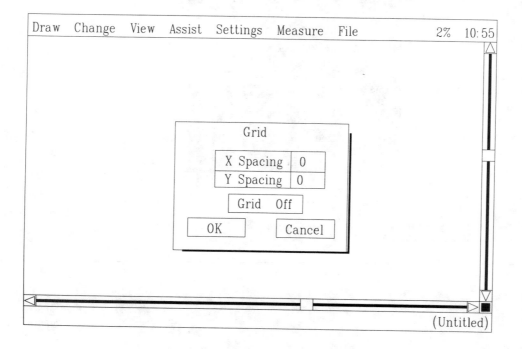

The Attach Command

In Unit 9 you learned to use the Assist menu for toggling the Attach command on and off. With the Settings menu, you select the Attach command and a dialogue box appears. You then set up the method AutoSketch uses to connect lines, circles, and arcs to other elements as you draw and edit. Let's see how the Attach setting works.

pp. 10-17

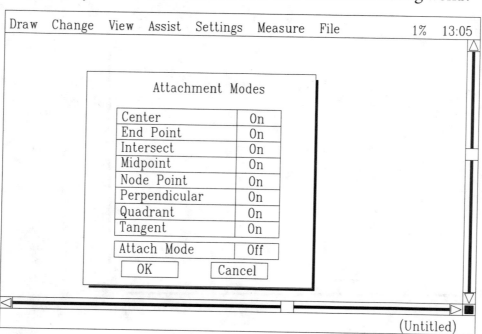

Midpoint

1. Load AutoSketch.

2. Select the **Settings** menu and the **Attach** command.

3. Toggle the Attach Mode **On**.

▶ *Hint:*

> Remember that you can also turn Attach on or off by using the Attach command on the Assist menu.

4. Turn off all the attach modes except **Midpoint**.

5. Close the dialogue box.

Let's say you want to draw the T below with a horizontal and a vertical bar. If you try to draw the horizontal bar exactly centered over the vertical bar, you need to take several steps. With the Attach mode, you can do the same drawing much more easily. Let's give it a try.

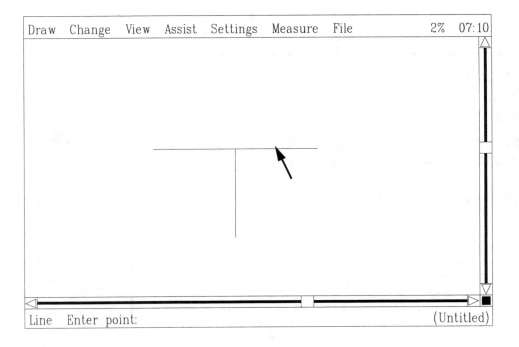

6. Draw the horizontal line of a T.

7. Touch the pointer anywhere on the horizontal line to select the first point of the vertical line.

8. Select the second point of the line.

The vertical line should be connected to the horizontal line at the exact midpoint. You can see how using the attach modes speeds up the drawing process.

AutoSketch®
Reference
Manual
p. 115

Endpoint

The End Point attach mode connects drawing elements to the endpoints of other lines or arcs. Just select a point close to the endpoint of a drawing element. AutoSketch will attach the element you are drawing at the exact endpoint.

AutoSketch®
Reference
Manual
p. 78

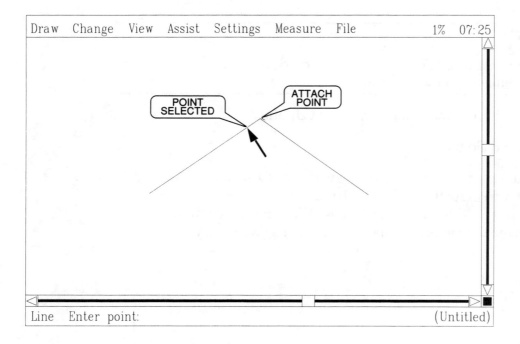

Quadrant

The Quadrant attach mode lets you attach elements to a point exactly one-fourth of the distance around a circle or an arc.

p. 166

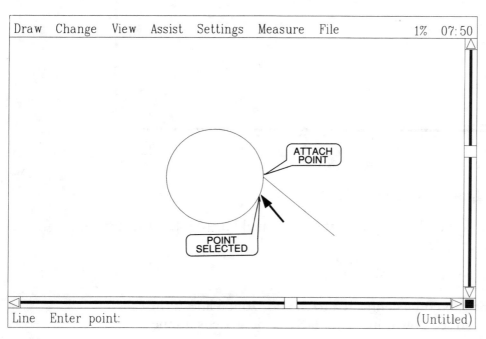

Center

The Center attach mode is used to connect a drawing element to the center of a circle or an arc. All you have to do is select the edge of the circle or arc, and AutoSketch will find the center for you. Without the Circle Attach mode, drawing circles that have the same center point is much harder. You would have to enter the coordinates of the center point or use the Snap command.

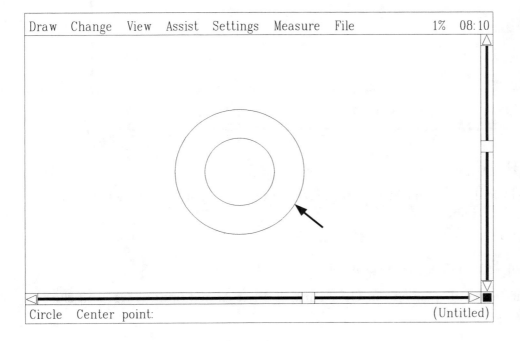

| Draw | Change | View | Assist | Settings | Measure | File | | 1% | 08:10 |

Circle   Center point: (Untitled)

Intersect

The Intersect option of the Attach command is used to connect an object at the intersection of two existing objects.

p. 101

1.   Select the **Attach** command.

2.   Turn the **Intersect** option **On**. Turn the other Attach options **Off**.

3.   Check to see that the Attach Mode is **On** and close the dialogue box.

4.   Draw two intersecting lines.

5.   Select the **Circle** command from the **Draw** menu.

6.   Select a point near the intersection of the two lines.

You will see the circle that will be drawn. If you have chosen a point close enough to the intersection, the center will be the intersection of the two lines.

7.   Select the second point for the circle.

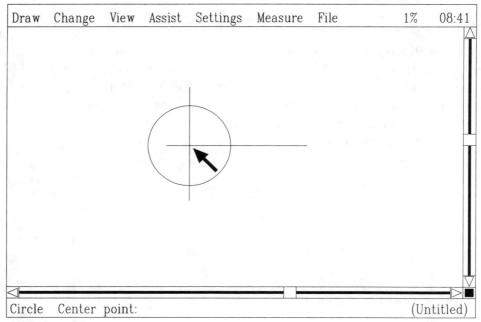

Draw   Change   View   Assist   Settings   Measure   File   1%   08:41

Circle   Center point: (Untitled)

Perpendicular

The Perpendicular option of the Attach command allows you to draw a line at a 90°
angle to an existing line.

1.   Draw a line.

2.   Select the **Settings** menu and the **Attach** command.

3.   Turn the Perpendicular option **On**. Turn all other Attach options **Off** and close
the dialogue box.

4.   To draw the second line, pick a point anywhere on the existing line.

You will see a perpendicular line that you can move until you decide where you want to
place it.

5.   Select the place where you want the line to appear.

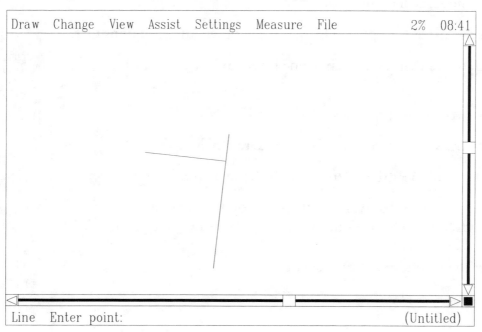

Line   Enter point: (Untitled)

Tangent

The Tangent option of the Attach menu allows you to create a line tangent to a circle or arc. A line that is tangent is drawn so that it touches one point on the edge of the circle or arc. If you drew a line perpendicular (at a 90° angle) to the tangent line, the line will always cross the center of the circle.

1. Draw one small circle and one large circle.

2. Select the **Settings** menu and the **Attach** command.

3. Turn the Tangent option **On**. Turn all other Attach options **Off** and close the dialogue box.

4. Select the **Line** command from the **Draw** menu.

5. Pick the upper part of the larger circle.

6. Pick the upper part of the small circle.

The line will connect to both circles.

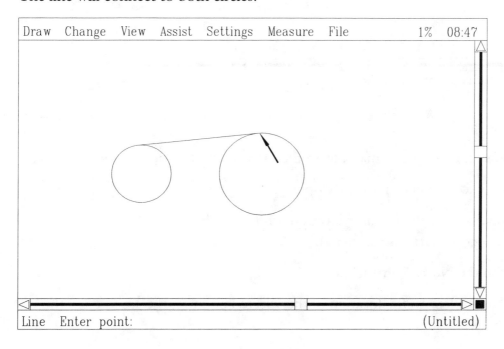

Node Point

The last Attach mode option is the Node Point. With this mode turned on, you can connect objects to points that you created with the Point command on the Draw menu.

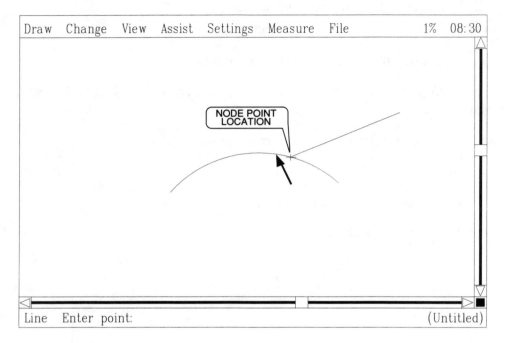

1. Draw an arc.

2. Then use the Point command from the Draw menu to place a point on the arc.

3. Now try to connect a line to that point.

It's hard to select exactly the same location, isn't it?

4. Now select the **Attach** command.

5. Turn on the **Node Point** feature.

6. Now move close to the location of the selected point on the arc to draw the connecting line.

AutoSketch will find the point you selected before.

▶ *Hint:*

You must point within an unseen boundary determined by the pick interval. You will learn what the pick interval is and how to change it in the next section about the Pick command.

✓✓ Exercise 1

With the Attach modes in operation, you can select the center of a circle and the midpoint of a line quickly and accurately. The attach modes make it easy. Follow the steps to create the drawing shown here.

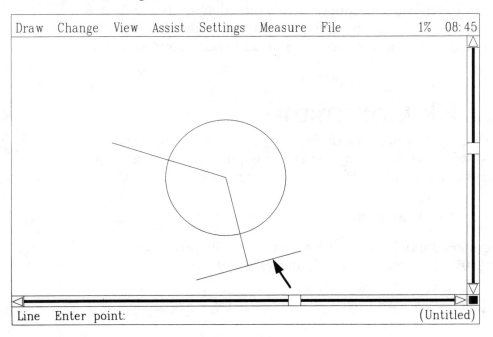

1. Draw the circle and the first line as shown below.

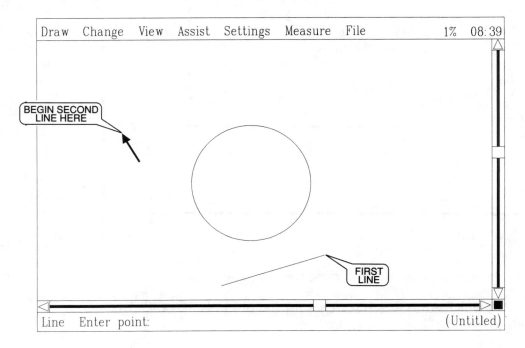

2. Turn off all but the **Midpoint** and **Center Attach** modes.

3. Begin a second line as shown.

4. Select any point on the edge of the circle.

The line will attach to the center.

5.   Use the **Attach** mode to begin a third line by attaching it to the
      center of the circle. Then connect it to the midpoint of the first
      line.

What happens if you draw with all the attach modes turned on at
once? AutoSketch will select attach points according to the element you
are drawing. It chooses center and quadrant points for circles and arcs,
midpoints and endpoints for lines and arcs, and node points for other
elements.

The Pick Command

pp. 143 -
144

How far does AutoSketch look for objects to attach drawing elements
to? The distance is set up using the Pick dialogue box and is determined
on the basis of a percentage of the screen height. Let's look at an
example.

1.   Select the **Pick** command.

The pick interval should be 1, which means 1%. Suppose the screen
height is 9.0". That means the pick interval is .09".

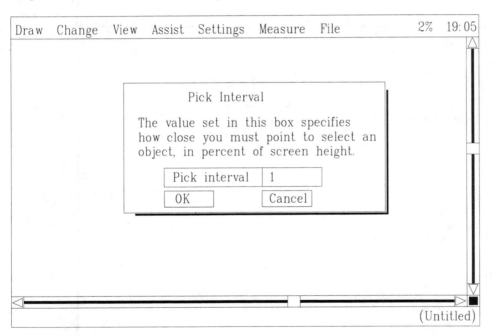

```
Draw   Change   View   Assist   Settings   Measure   File        2%   19:05


                     Pick Interval

          The value set in this box specifies
          how close you must point to select an
          object, in percent of screen height.

              Pick interval    1
               OK                 Cancel


                                                          (Untitled)
```

2.   Enter a pick interval of **3** and close the dialogue box.

The zone in which AutoSketch searches for the object is 3% of 9", or
.27". Now try attaching to an endpoint.

3.   Draw a line.

4.   Select the **End Point** mode on the **Attach** command.

5.   Pick a point on the drawing that is about 1/2" from the line. Do
      not pick a point on the line.

Does the new line attach to the original?

6. Change the pick interval to **20.**

7. Once again, try to connect a line to the endpoint, staying about 1/2" away.

This time the lines should connect, since the pick interval is larger.

8. Change the pick interval back to 1.

*AutoSketch®
Reference
Manual*

▶ *Hint:*

When you draw in small areas you will need a small pick zone. In that case, lower the percentage entered in the Pick dialogue box.

The Chamfer Command

As you learned in Unit 7, the Chamfer command on the Change menu creates a beveled edge on an existing object. With the Settings menu, you change the size of the chamfer and the angle with a dialogue box like the one below.

pp. 32-37

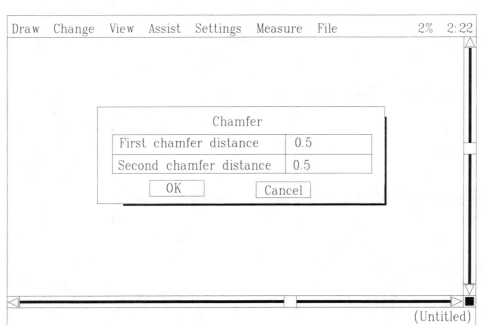

```
Draw   Change   View   Assist   Settings   Measure   File          2%   2:22
```

Chamfer	
First chamfer distance	0.5
Second chamfer distance	0.5

OK   Cancel

(Untitled)

AutoSketch uses the first chamfer distance to locate the first leg of the chamfer and the second distance to select the second leg. The angle depends upon the length of the two legs.

1. Draw an object with a chamfer on one corner.

2. Select the **Settings** menu and the **Chamfer** command.

3. Select new sizes for the dialogue box.

4. Draw a new chamfer on the object.

AutoSketch®
Reference
Manual

▶ *Hint:*

You can use a crosses/window box to select two corner lines at
once. When two or more lines appear in the box, AutoSketch
decides which lines are first and second. If the distances you choose
are different values, use the hand pointer. That way, you can decide
the direction of the chamfer.

The Fillet Command

As you know, the Fillet command is like the Chamfer command
(Unit 7). With the Settings menu you can insert the radius you want
with a dialogue box like the one below.

pp. 88-93

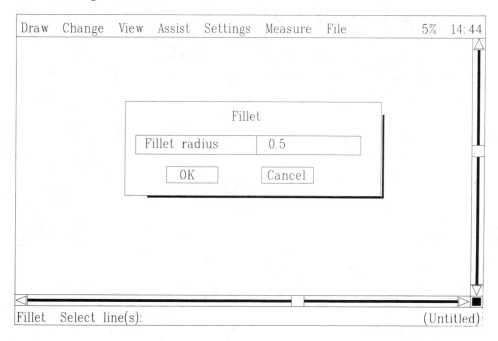

To give it a try, follow these steps.

1. Draw an object with a fillet on one corner.

2. Select the **Fillet** command.

3. Select a new radius for the dialogue box.

4. Add a new fillet with the new setting.

▶ *Hint:*

If the radius is set to 0°, the corner will look the same as it did before
you used the Fillet command. You can also use this command to
trim intersecting lines by setting the radius to zero.

The Box Array Command

AutoSketch®
Reference
Manual
pp. 20-27

The Box Array command in the Change menu creates rows and columns of objects (Unit 7). The same command under the Settings menu allows you to change the way the array works while you draw.

The dialogue box below appears on the screen when you select the Box Array command. You then change the distances between the rows and columns, as well as the number of rows and columns you want.

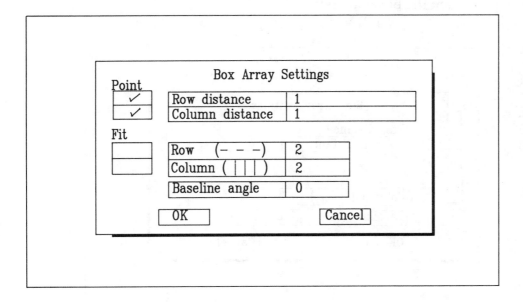

The first choice you have is to select row and column distances. If a check mark appears in the Point box, you will change the distance with the hand pointer. If you turn off the Point box, AutoSketch automatically spaces the array object on the screen according to the values in the dialogue box. Let's try changing the values.

1. Draw a small object in the lower left corner of the screen.

2. Select the **Settings** menu and the **Box Array** command.

The default settings for row and column distance are both 1 unit.

3. Enter **3** for the **Row Distance** and **3** for the **Column Distance.**

When you enter a new value, the Point box is automatically turned off. Now you can decide how many rows and columns you want.

4. Enter new values for the **Rows** and **Columns** boxes.

5. Close the dialogue box.

6. Select the **Change** menu and the **Box Array** command.

7. Select the object.

AutoSketch creates rows and columns of the original object. A dialogue box appears asking if you want to accept or modify the array.

8.   Select **Modify**.

Another way to select row and column distances is with the Fit box. With the box on, AutoSketch fits an array into an area outlined by the distances you have chosen in the **Row Distance** and the **Column Distance** boxes.

9.   Turn both **Fit** boxes on.

Check marks appear when the boxes are on.

```
                        Box Array Settings
  Point
  ┌─────────┐    ┌──────────────────┬─────┐
  │         │    │ Row  distance    │ 1   │
  │         │    │ Column distance  │ 1   │
  └─────────┘    └──────────────────┴─────┘
  Fit
  ┌─────────┐    ┌──────────────────┬─────┐
  │   ✓     │    │ Rows    (– – –)  │ 10  │
  │   ✓     │    │ Column  ( │ │ │ )│ 5   │
  └─────────┘    ├──────────────────┼─────┤
                 │ Baseline angle   │ 0   │
                 └──────────────────┴─────┘
        ┌──────┐              ┌────────┐
        │  OK  │              │ Cancel │
        └──────┘              └────────┘
```

10. Close the dialogue box.

Did your array change?

   Now you can choose a baseline angle. Imagine a line drawn along the bottom of the array. That is the baseline angle. Changing this setting will move the baseline of the array to the angle that you enter. The default setting is 0°, and you can select any angle between 0° and 360°. For example, if you choose an angle of 60°, the entire array of objects on the screen will move 60°. The individual objects, on the other hand, stay the same way you drew them. All degree settings are in a counter-clockwise direction, starting with 0° at the three o'clock position.

11. Open the dialogue box.

12. Enter a new angle.

13. Close the dialogue box.

   You will probably want to experiment with this command to take better advantage of its power.

The Ring Array Command

*AutoSketch®
Reference
Manual*
pp. 169-174

As you learned in Unit 7, the Ring Array command in the Change menu creates a circular pattern of objects. For the Settings menu, this command provides a dialogue box, like the one below, to help you set up the circular array.

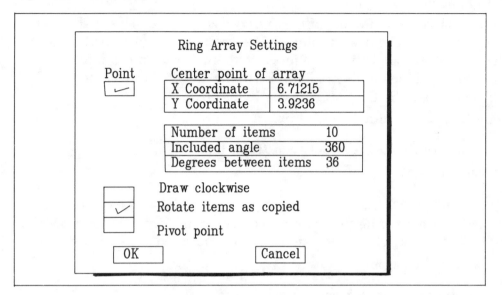

The settings you can change are

- the center point
- the number of objects
- the angle and degrees between the objects
- the way the object is rotated

Your first choice from the dialogue box is to select the center point of the array. If a check mark appears in the Point box, you will change the center point with the hand pointer. If you turn off the Point box, AutoSketch automatically places the center of the array on the screen according to the values in the dialogue box. Try changing the values by following these steps.

1. Draw a small object on the screen.

Leave enough room for an array.

2. Select the **Ring Array** command.

3. Enter new values for the **X Coordinate** and **Y Coordinate** and close the dialogue box.

4. Select the **Change** menu and the **Ring Array** command.

5. Select the object.

The new array should be centered at the coordinates you chose. You should also see a dialogue box asking if you want to accept or modify the array.

6. Select **Modify.**

Now you can change the number of items.

7. Enter a new value for the **Number of Items** box.

Because this is a circular array, you can also decide the angle between objects. The angle can be set in one of two ways.

The first method is to choose a value for the *Included Angle* box. This angle sets up the size of the arc or circle. The default value of 360° creates a complete circle. AutoSketch then divides the angle by the number of items. For example, if the included angle is 360° and the number of items is 10, the degrees between items is 36. AutoSketch will enter 36 in the Degrees Between Items box.

8. Enter an angle in the **Included Angle** box.

What is the new value for the **Degrees Between Items** box?

9. Close the dialogue box.

What happened to your array?

The second method of changing the angle is to enter a value for the Degrees Between Items box. AutoSketch will then figure out the included angle for you.

10. Open the dialogue box again.

11. Enter a new number in the **Degrees Between Items** box.

If you enter a number that is too large, AutoSketch will not accept it. Do you have a new included angle?

The next three choices set up the way the array is rotated. A check mark will appear when you have selected one of these options.

First, the Draw Clockwise box draws the objects in the array in a clockwise direction. The usual way for AutoSketch to draw is in the counterclockwise direction.

Next is the Rotate Items as Copied box. This box sets up the way the individual objects are rotated. If you select this box, AutoSketch turns each object in relation to the center of the array. If you turn this box off, AutoSketch copies each object the way you drew it in the first place.

The next choice is the Pivot Point box. This box lets you select the point around which the objects will rotate. When you choose this option, the Rotate Items as Copied box is automatically turned off.

Experiment with these choices to see how they affect an array.

The Curve Command

AutoSketch®
Reference
Manual
pp. 50-53

    With the Curve dialogue box, you control the precision that AutoSketch uses to create curves. The more drawing segments entered, the smoother the curve will be.

1.   Select the **Curve** command from the **Settings** menu.

What is the number of segments between control points that AutoSketch normally uses to draw curves? The answer is 8.

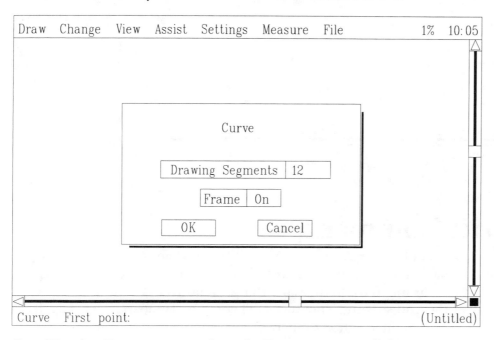

2.   Use the **Curve** command on the **Draw** menu to make a curve.

3.   Now use the **Curve** Command on the **Settings** menu to reduce the drawing segments value to 4.

    AutoSketch will redraw the curve. Does it look different? You entered fewer segments, so the curve is probably not as smooth.

    You have probably noticed another feature in the Curve dialogue box. You can also use the box to turn the Frame feature on or off.

▶ *Hint:*

As you learned in Unit 9, the Frame command on the Assist menu also toggles the frame around a curve on or off. Remember that when you need to see the points that AutoSketch will use to make the curve, you can make this frame visible by using the Frame command on either the Assist menu or the Settings menu.

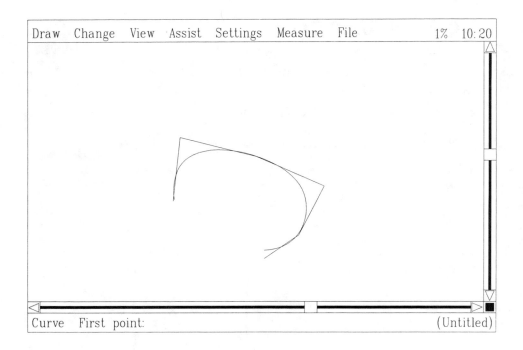

The Grid Command

With the Grid command on the Assist menu (Unit 9), you can make the grid appear or disappear on the drawing area. You can use the Grid command on the Settings menu to do the same thing. This dialogue box also lets you set the grid spacing. The values tell you how far apart in drawing units the grid points are horizontally (X spacing) and vertically (Y spacing).

Let's try using it.

1.   Select the **Grid** command.

pp. 96 - 98

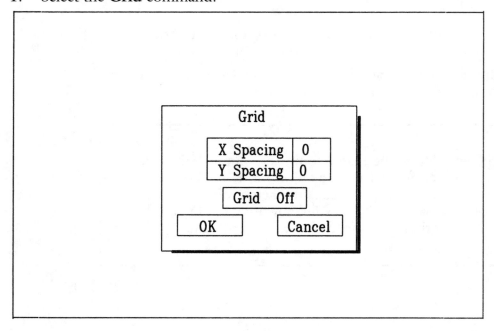

What spacing does AutoSketch normally use for the grid? The dialogue box says either 0,0 or 1,1. If the grid spacing is 0,0, AutoSketch automatically uses snap values for grid spacing, too. Since AutoSketch normally uses snap values of 1,1, the grid spacing is really 1,1.

2.   Turn the grid on.

3.   Close the dialogue box.

The grid should cover the drawing area; its points should be evenly spaced, 1 drawing unit apart.

4.   Now bring up the **Grid** dialogue box as you did in step 1.

5.   Change the X-axis spacing to **.5** and the Y-axis spacing to **.25.**

Notice that the Y-axis value is changed to equal the X-axis value unless you enter different values for each axis.

6.   Close the dialogue box.

How does the grid look now? It should look like the one below.

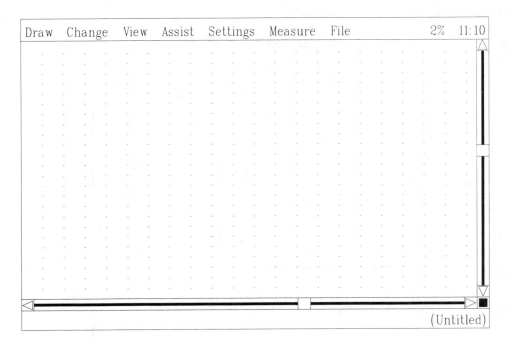

You can change the spacing of the grid at any time while you are drawing with AutoSketch.

The Snap Command

The Snap feature causes a small cross to jump to snap points. You can turn on Snap with a command on the Assist menu or the Settings menu. The same command on the Settings menu is used to tell AutoSketch what points to use as snap points. The Snap feature allows you to draw with accuracy.

pp. 185 -
187

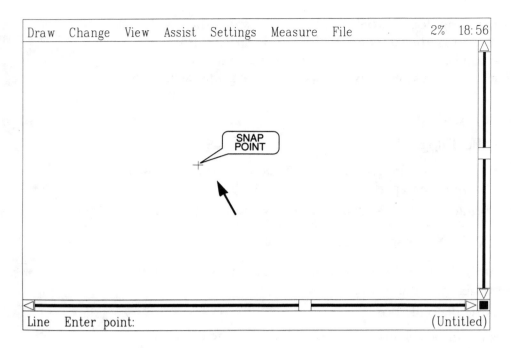

1. To make it easier to see the snap distances, turn on the grid.

2. Select the **Snap** command and make sure **Snap** is turned on.

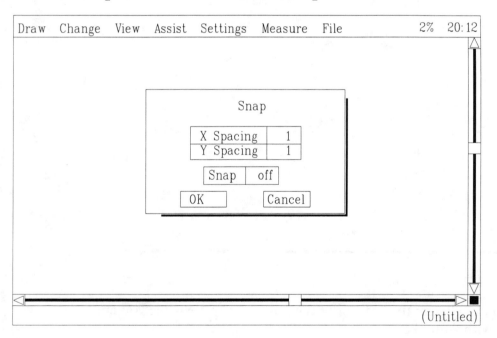

3. Close the dialogue box.

4. Move your pointer around the screen.

You can see the jerky movement as the pointer bounces from one snap point to another. With Snap turned on, the screen is divided into equal sections. You can select only the snap point within each section. This feature lets you draw elements that are exact lengths.

Suppose you want to draw a line that is 3.5" long, and you are using 1 drawing unit to represent 1 inch.

156 ■ The Settings Menu

1. Bring up the dialogue box.

2. Set the X-axis snap value to **.5** and pick **OK**.

3. Close the dialogue box.

4. Use the **Line** command to select the first point of the line.

5. Now move the small cross seven times, using the grid to keep track of the moves, and select the final location to finish the line.

Since 7 x .5 = 3.5, you have drawn a line that represents 3.5".

**AutoSketch®
Reference
Manual**

► *Hint:*

> Remember that the distance between snap points must relate to the size of your drawing area. If your drawing area is large and the snap distances are small, you won't have control over the Snap feature. But if your drawing area is small and snap distances are large, you will only have a few snap points that you can select on the screen. A good guide to follow is to set snap distances to the smallest unit of measure that you plan to use in the drawing. If you can't control the pointer, then make the snap distance twice as long.

The Part Base Command

The Part command on the Draw menu can be used to move a previously created drawing into a new drawing. The Part Base command on the Settings menu is used to mark the point for the part insertion base. AutoSketch uses this point to insert the original drawing into a new one.

pg. 124 - 129

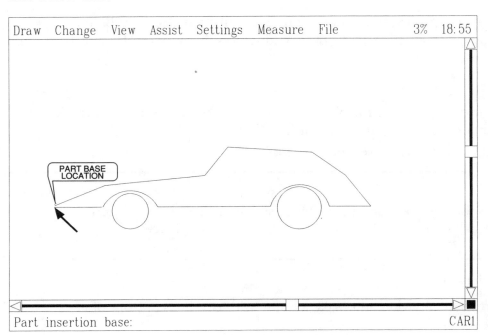

1. If you stored the car you drew in Unit 7, open that file, or draw a car.

2. Select the **Part Base** command from the **Settings** Menu.

The dialogue box for this command gives you several choices for setting up a part insertion base. The top section of the menu is for entering coordinates for this point through the keyboard. The lower section has two choices. The first sets the insertion base according to a default base point. The default base point is a point you pick on the screen. The second choice is used with the Part Clip command under the File menu.

Let's try the Default Base Point option.

3. Toggle the Default Base Point option **On**.

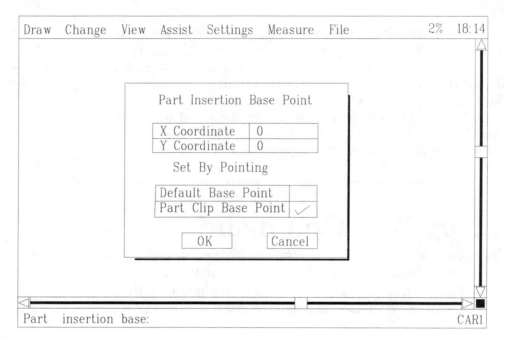

When a check mark appears, the option is on. Note that the Part Clip Base Point is also on by default. It will not actually do anything now, because the Default Base Point overrides it.

4. Close the dialogue box.

Next you will select a point for the part insertion base. You can use your pointing device or enter coordinates on the keyboard.

5. Pick a point for the part insertion base location.

▶ *Hint:*

Good choices for this point are the center of symmetrical objects (objects that can be divided in half evenly) or the lower left corner of other objects.

6. Save the drawing.

7. Now start a new drawing and make a house with two lines in front of it for a street.

Let's put the car on the street.

8.   Select the **Draw** menu and the **Part** command.

The dialogue box shows the drawings you have saved.

9.   Select the drawing where you saved the car.

10.   Close the dialogue box.

11.   Now move your pointing device along the street until you find a good location for the car.

Notice as you drag the car that your pointer is "attached" to the point you picked in step 5.

12.   Pick a location for the car.

The car drawing is now a part of your new drawing.

▶ # *Hint:*

Remember that AutoSketch draws the part in the new drawing without changing its properties. The layer, color, and line type will be the same as they were when you last saved the part drawing.

You can also use the top section of the Part Base dialogue box to enter coordinates for the part insertion base. You enter the new coordinates and close the dialogue box. You enter nothing on the screen; AutoSketch will automatically use those coordinates for the part insertion base.

You will practice the last option, Part Clip Base Point, in Unit 12 because this option is used with the Part Clip command under the File menu.

The Ellipse Command

The Ellipse command on the Settings menu is used to change the way you draw an ellipse with the same command on the Draw menu. As you may remember, an ellipse has a center point and two axes. The two axes intersect at the center point of the ellipse and are 90° apart.

pp. 72 - 77

| Draw   Change   View   Assist   Settings   Measure   File   29%   12:00 |

AXIS

AXIS

CENTER POINT

Ellipse   Center of ellipse: (Untitled)

There are three choices when you select the Ellipse command on the Settings menu. The first choice is Center and Both Axes, which is the default method. With this method, you choose the center point plus two points–one for each axis endpoint (Unit 7).

```
Draw   Change   View   Assist   Settings   Measure   File        0%   11:50



                    ┌─────────────────────────────────┐
                    │     Ellipse Input Format         │
                    │                                  │
                    │   ┌──────────────────────┬───┐   │
                    │   │ Center and Both Axes │   │   │
                    │   │ Axis and Planar Rotation │ │  │
                    │   │ Two Foci and Point   │   │   │
                    │   └──────────────────────┴───┘   │
                    │                                  │
                    │    ┌────────┐    ┌────────┐       │
                    │    │   OK   │    │ Cancel │       │
                    │    └────────┘    └────────┘       │
                    └─────────────────────────────────┘



                                                        (Untitled)
```

Axis and Planar Rotation

The second choice for the Ellipse command is Axis and Planer Rotation. When you select this option, you choose a center point for the ellipse and the endpoint of one axis. The next point determines what the ellipse will look like. Let's give this one a try.

1. Select the **Ellipse** command from the **Settings** menu.

2. Toggle the Axis and Planar Rotation option **On**.

3. Close the dialogue box.

4. Select the **Ellipse** command from the **Draw** menu.

5. Pick a point on the screen for the center point.

6. Pick a point to the right for the endpoint of the first axis.

7. Move the pointer around the screen.

You will see what the ellipse might look like when you choose the last point. The last point rotates around the center point. The angle of rotation is measured from this point to the first axis.

This ellipse is like drawing a circle on a sheet of paper and rotating the paper so that it is no longer flat. As you rotate the paper, the circle begins to look like an ellipse.

8. Choose the last point.

p. 74

Two Foci and Point

The last choice under the Ellipse command is Two Foci and Point. With this option, you choose the first and second foci (plural of focus) of the ellipse and then a point on the ellipse. The foci of an ellipse are two points along the first axis.

AutoSketch®
Reference
Manual
pp. 75 - 76

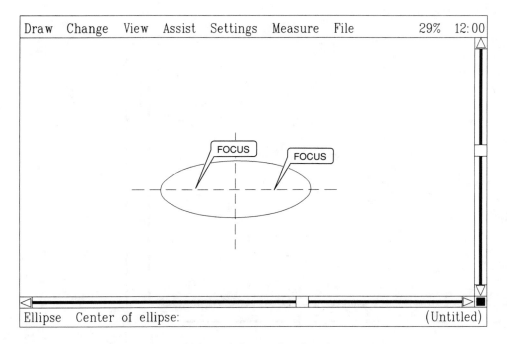

1. Select the **Ellipse** command from the **Settings** menu.

2. Turn the Two Foci and Point option **On.**

3. Select **Ellipse** from the **Draw** menu.

4. Select a point for the first focus.

5. Select a point for the second focus.

These two points determine the length of the axis and the size of the ellipse. As you move the pointing device, you will see a temporary view of the new ellipse. Note that two lines connect the foci to the outer edge of the ellipse. As you move the pointing device away from the foci, the ellipse will change shape from flat to circular.

6. Select the third point for the ellipse.

The Text Command

AutoSketch®
Reference
Manual
pp. 192 -
209

The Text command brings up the Text and Font Modes dialogue box. You may recognize this dialogue box from Unit 7. This dialogue box is the same one you see when you select the Settings option of the Text command under the Change menu. All of the functions are the same as the ones you tried out in Unit 7.

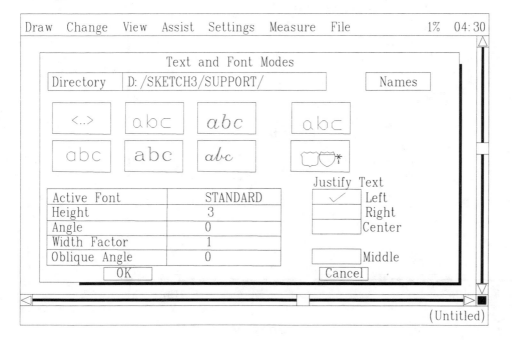

The Layer Command

pp. 102 -
105

Besides changing the way the drawing and editing commands work, you can also change properties of drawings using Settings commands. One of these properties is layer.

You probably remember from Unit 7 that layers of a CAD drawing are like transparent overlays of a paper drawing. You can draw some objects on one layer of a drawing and save others for other layers. By printing or plotting different layers, you can show only as much detail of a drawing as you need.

In an engineering office, this feature is useful. The engineer can plot just the drawing elements that suppliers of parts need without giving away secrets of the design of an entire machine. Also, the details are more readable on a separate layer than they would be on the whole drawing.

You can also put on a separate layer the points that you used in a drawing just for locating or measuring elements. Then you can print or plot the drawing without showing those points.

You can change the layer on which you are drawing by using the Layer command on the Settings menu.

1.   Draw a robot like the one below.

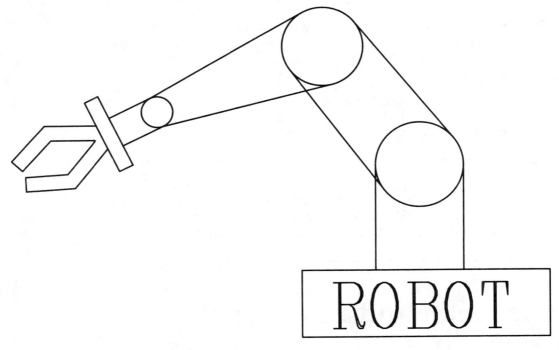

2.   Now bring up the **Layer** dialogue box.

Which drawing layer is current? AutoSketch always places elements on Layer 1 when you start a new drawing.

3.   Now make Layer 6 current by toggling that layer **On**.

Notice that the check mark moves from the Layer 1 box to the Layer 6 box. Only one layer can be current at a time.

4.   Close the dialogue box.

5.   Now draw an object. For example, you might draw an object that the robot is lifting.

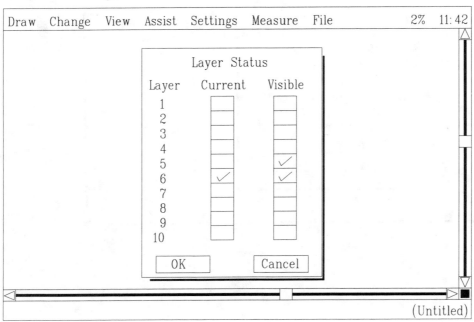

With ten layers to choose from, you would have enough room to completely fill the screen with details.

Besides drawing on different layers, you can also change which layers are displayed on the screen (or plotted on paper). You know how to turn layers on and off. Now let's see how to make them visible and invisible.

*AutoSketch®
Reference
Manual*

6.   Select the **Layer** command again.

7.   Toggle Layer 6 off to make it invisible.

▶ *Hint:*

If you forget which layer you have used to draw an element, you can find out by using the Show Properties command on the Measure menu. You will read more about this command in Unit 11.

The Color and Line Type Commands

The Color command lets you change the color AutoSketch uses as you add elements to a drawing. Or you can use different colors on different layers to separate elements in a complicated drawing. The colors you select can be used for pens in plotting your drawing. So even if you don't have a color monitor, you can assign colors to different elements in a drawing in order to plot them.

pp. 41 - 43

pp. 108 - 109

```
Draw   Change   View   Assist   Settings   Measure   File        1%   09:10



                         Drawing Color

                    ┌─────────────┬──────┬─────────┐
                    │ Red         │      │ ─────── │
                    │ Yellow      │      │ ─────── │
                    │ Green       │      │ ─────── │
                    │ Cyan        │      │ ─────── │
                    │ Blue        │      │ ─────── │
                    │ Magenta     │      │ ─────── │
                    │ Black       │  ✓   │ ─────── │
                    └─────────────┴──────┴─────────┘

                    ┌──────────────────┬──────┐
                    │ Color Number     │   7  │
                    └──────────────────┴──────┘
                    ┌──────────┐    ┌──────────┐
                    │   OK     │    │  Cancel  │
                    └──────────┘    └──────────┘


                                                      (Untitled)
```

Another way of separating elements in a drawing is changing the line type that AutoSketch uses to draw them. Besides choosing the combination of dots and dashes, you can also change the amount of space AutoSketch leaves between them. You can enter a new scale factor in the dialogue box. Unless you change this value, AutoSketch spaces dots or dashes 0.5 drawing unit apart.

AutoSketch®
Reference
Manual

▶ *Hint:*

Text and dimensions (measurements) can only be shown in solid line type.

Draw	Change	View	Assist	Settings	Measure	File	3%	17:35

Drawing Line Type

Solid		———————
Dashed		— — — — —
Hidden		— — — — — —
Center		— — — — —
Phantom		— — — —
Dot		··················
Dashdot		— · — · — ·
Border		— — — —
Divide		— · · — · · — ·
Dots		— — — — — ·

Scale factor | 0.5

OK   Cancel

Line   Enter point: (Untitled)

The Property Command

In Unit 7, you practiced changing properties of drawing elements as part of editing a drawing. To choose which properties to change, use the Property command on the Settings menu. A Change Property Modes dialogue box will tell you what properties are currently in use.

pp. 164 -
165

▶ *Hint:*

If you want to make changes, bring up the Settings menu dialogue box for each property and set up new values. Then you can use the Property command on the Change menu to select elements in your drawing that you want changed.

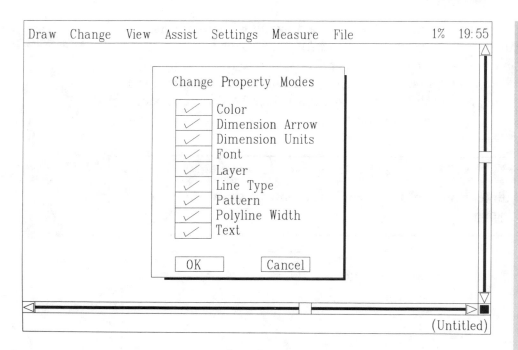

AutoSketch®
Reference
Manual

The Limits Command

The Limits command is used to enlarge or shrink your drawing area as you use the Grid and Zoom features of AutoSketch. You do this by changing the drawing limits, as you practiced in Unit 8 with the Zoom Limits command. A dialogue box is shown on the next page.

pp. 105 - 107

The best way to set limits is to use values that represent a size close to the paper size you will plot your drawing on. That way you will draw only within the area shown on the screen, and everything you draw will fit on the paper you use to plot.

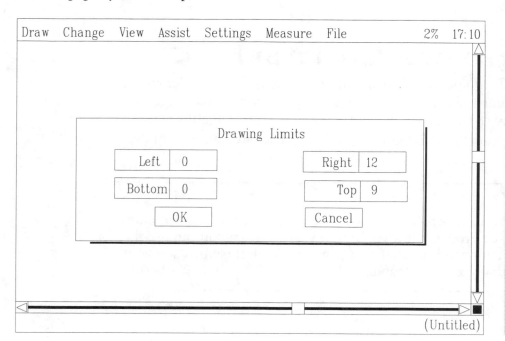

► *Hint:*

To compensate for plotter track wheels, set the lower left limit corner to a negative number. For example, if you want the corner of your plotted drawing to correspond to point 0,0, use -1 for the X and Y values of the lower left limits. In other words, set the Left box to -1 and the Bottom box to -1. You can set the upper right limits at any value, as long as the value is not the same as or less than the value of the lower left limits.

The Units Command

The Units Command provides a dialogue box for setting the type of dimensions, or measurements displayed, while using AutoSketch. The two choices are Decimal or Architectural. Under each choice are options for setting precision values. The default settings for AutoSketch are the Decimal and three Digits boxes.

pp. 210 - 213

```
Draw   Change   View   Assist   Settings   Measure   File          2%   14:41

                        Units  Display  Format

        Decimal                      Architectural   ✓
                          Precision
        0  digits                    1/1"
        1  digit                     1/2"
        2  digits                    1/4"
        3  digits                    1/8"   ✓
        4  digits    ✓               1/16"
        5  digits                    1/32"
        6  digits                    1/64"

                   Decimal  suffix

                OK              Cancel

                                                              (Untitled)
```

You can also add a suffix if you are using decimal units. A suffix is a label like in. (inches) or ft. (feet).

To change an existing unit, select the Property command under the Settings menu. Make sure the Dimension Units box is selected. Then apply the new type of unit with the Change menu, Property command.

The Pattern Command

The Pattern Command works with the Pattern Fill command on the Draw menu. When you create a pattern-filled object, the default pattern appears, unless you first set up a different pattern on the Settings menu.

pp. 129 - 140

This command also works with the Property command on the Change menu to change a pattern-filled object that you have already drawn.

First try creating new objects with patterns set up on the Settings menu.

1. Select the **Settings** menu and the **Pattern** command.

A dialogue box appears with icons of various types of patterns to choose from.

2. Use the scroll bar to view the different types of patterns.

3. Pick an icon and close the dialogue box.

You have selected a new pattern. When you draw an object, it will be filled with this pattern.

4. Select the **Pattern Fill** command from the **Draw** menu.

5. Draw an object.

6. Select the **Accept** box

Now try changing a pattern.

7. Make several copies of the object you have already drawn.

8. Select the **Settings** menu and the **Pattern** command.

9. Select a new pattern and close the dialogue box.

Before you apply the new change, use the Property command on the Settings menu.

10. Select the **Settings**, **Property** command.

11. Make sure that the Pattern option is selected.

12. Select the **Change** menu and the **Property** command.

13. Select one of the objects.

The object will fill with the new pattern.

14. Select and apply a new pattern for each of the objects on the screen.

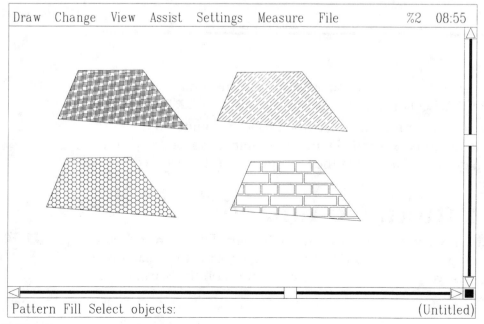

There are several other options for setting up patterns with the Pattern Settings dialogue box. Some of the choices change depending upon which pattern you have chosen. One option that applies to all the patterns is the Boundary box to the right (below the scroll bar). If you turn this box off, the boundary of the object will not appear.

The Polyline Command

The Polyline command on the Settings menu works with the Polyline command on the Draw menu. With this command, you can change the width or appearance of a line drawn with the Polyline command.

1. Select the **Polyline** command from the **Settings** menu.

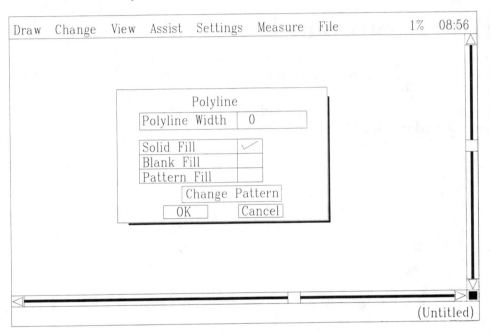

AutoSketch®
Reference
Manual

pp. 158 -
163

2. Set the Polyline Width to **.1** and close the dialogue box.

3. Select the **Polyline** command from the **Draw** menu.

4. Draw a line.

If you have drawn a line with Polyline, you can use the Property command on the Settings menu and the Polyline command on the Change menu to change to a new width. Now try out the other Polyline options by changing the line you have drawn.

5. Select **Polyline** from the **Settings** menu.

6. Turn the Blank Fill box **On** and close the dialogue box.

7. Select the Property command on the Settings Menu and make sure Polyline width is selected.

8. Select the **Property** command on the **Change** menu.

9. Select the line on your screen.

How does the line look now?

10. Select **Settings** and **Polyline**.

11. Turn the Pattern Fill box **On**.

12. Set the Polyline Width to **1**.

13. Select the **Change Pattern** box.

14. Select the **STARS** pattern and close the dialogue boxes.

15. Use the Change menu to apply the new changes.

The Arrow Command

p. 9
pp. 63 - 64

The Arrow command on the Settings menu is used when you add dimensions to a drawing. With this option, you can choose the type of arrowhead that AutoSketch draws on the end of dimension lines placed on the drawing. Since dimensions are added with the Measure menu, these options are covered in Unit 11.

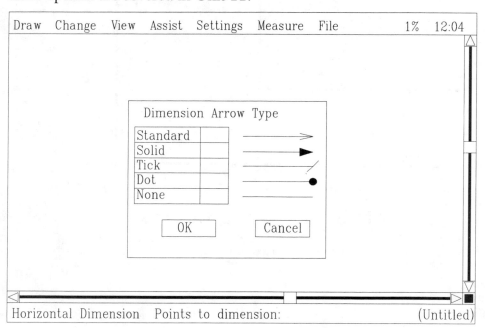

Key Terms

baseline angle   obliquing angle
included angle

Let's Review

 *Questions*

1. Name three of the attach modes you can use to connect points.

    _____

    _____

    _____

2. What is the Pick dialogue box used for?

    _____

    _____

3. Explain how the Curve command on the Settings menu changes the way the Curve command on the Draw menu works.

    _____

    _____

    _____

4. How is being able to change grid and snap spacing helpful in making drawings?

    _____

    _____

    _____

5. How does the Part base command on the Settings menu work with the Part command on the Draw menu?

    _____

    _____

    _____

6. Explain how choosing different drawing properties can make drawings more useful.

_____

_____

_____

7. What is a good guide to follow in setting drawing limits?

_____

_____

_____

8. Name three methods you can use to draw an ellipse.

_____

_____

_____

9. What is the Pattern command on the Settings menu used for?

_____

_____

_____

10. The Polyline command on the Settings menu works with which command on the Draw menu?

_____

_____

_____

Problems

1. Create a drawing similar to the one below. Use red color lines for the base and green for the upper section. Make all holes using the Hidden line type. When adding the text, use a height of .20, a width factor of .75, and an obliquing angle of 20 degrees.

Special alignment device for setting lens offsets

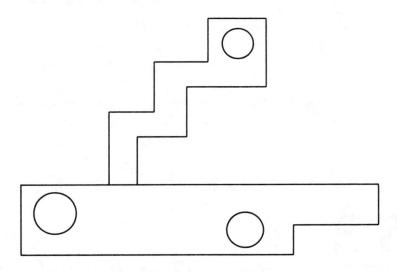

Note: No scale required

2. Create the following shape. Use a snap setting of .5 and the following Attach modes: Center, Quadrant, End Point, and Midpoint.

3. Set the snap mode to .5 and recreate the following figure. Then, imagine that each unit represents a scale of 1/4" = 1'-0". Set the lower corner limits to 0,0 and the upper right corner to 60,40. Use the Zoom limits commands to view the drawing within the new limits.

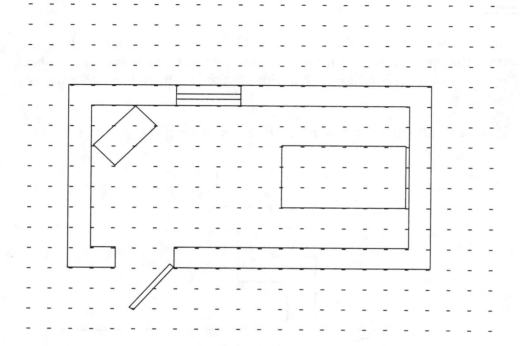

Extend Your Knowledge

1. Make up a logo to represent the class you are in or a symbol representing yourself. Use different colors to draw it out in rough form on paper. Then construct the logo with AutoSketch, using three or more layers with the different colors.

2. Draw a plain T-shirt on paper. Then create two or three designs for the shirt on transparent overlays. Creating overlays is like using the Layer command in AutoSketch.

3. Read about custom patterns in the *AutoSketch Reference Manual*, Appendix D, beginning on page 247. (This manual is provided with the AutoSketch software.) Sketch a new pattern on paper. Then create the new pattern with AutoSketch.

The Measure Menu

AutoSketch® Reference Manual

pp. 113 - 114

Objectives:

■ *Use Measure commands to find information about coordinates and properties of drawing elements.*

■ *To measure distances, angles, and area.*

■ *To use the dimensioning commands to measure elements of drawings.*

The Measure menu offers a variety of ways that you can measure parts of your drawings. AutoSketch records the exact locations of drawing elements as you create them on the drawing screen. Since AutoSketch

| Draw | Change | View | Assist | Settings | Measure | File | 2% 09:30 |

Angle
Area
Distance

Bearing
Point

Align dimension
Angle Dimension
Horiz. Dimension
Vert. Dimension

Show Properties

(Untitled)

can recall the location of specific points at any time, it can give you precise measurements in your drawings. That is why AutoSketch is such a powerful drawing tool. You won't need to use measuring tools as you draw.

AutoSketch®
Reference
Manual

p. 157

The Point Command

The simplest measuring device of AutoSketch is the Point command.

1. Load AutoSketch.

2. Select the **Point** command from the **Measure** menu.

3. Now roam around the screen with your pointing device in a pattern like the one shown on the drawing below.

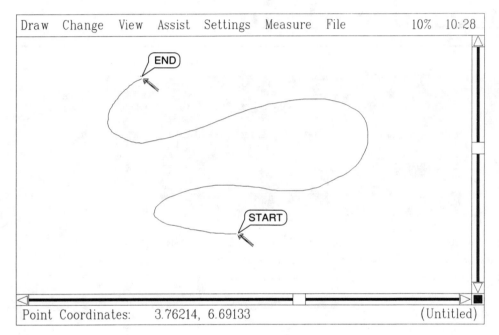

| Draw | Change | View | Assist | Settings | Measure | File | 10% | 10:28 |

Point Coordinates: 3.76214, 6.69133   (Untitled)

What appears in the lower left-hand corner of the screen?

The prompt reads "Point coordinates:" and is followed by the X- and Y-axis values for the location of your arrow pointer. As you move the pointer, the coordinate values change. When you select a point, a dialogue box like the one on the next page will be shown, telling you the exact coordinates of the location. You can also find out the coordinates of any location without picking it by carefully watching the prompt area and recording the information.

As you learned in Unit 6, there is also a Point command on the Draw menu. You can create points with the Draw menu and use them to help measure distances and bearings.

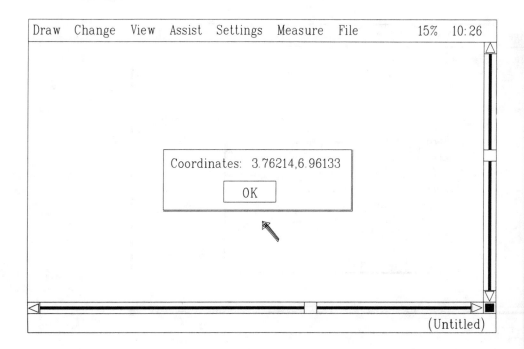

AutoSketch®
Reference
Manual

Hint:

The Point command can help you start or finish a line to get an exact fit as you draw.

The Show Properties Command

The Show Properties command is another feature of AutoSketch that gives you useful information as you draw. Let's try it out.

pp. 182 -
183

1. Pull the drawing ERICSON1 from your drawing files.

2. Select the **Show Properties** command.

The hand pointer will appear on the screen.

3. Select part of the sailboat, such as the bow or stern.

A dialogue box, similar to the one on the next page, will appear with information about the element you selected. You can find out properties such as the object type, layer number, color number and name, and line type. When you are creating a complicated drawing or looking at a drawing you made previously, this command can refresh your memory about how you planned to separate the elements by using different properties.

4. Select several parts of the drawing to see the different properties used.

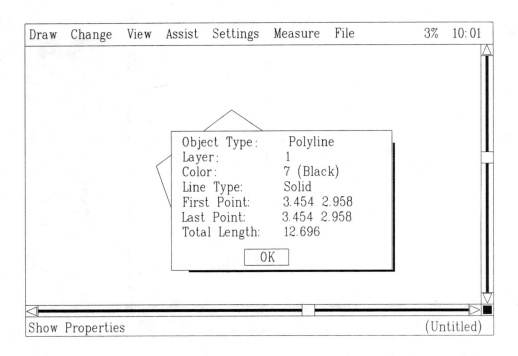

The Distance Command

Now you will start actually measuring items in drawings. The Distance command calculates the distance between two points.

pp. 65 - 66

1. Draw a line on the screen.

2. Turn on the **Endpoint** attach mode using the **Attach** command on the **Settings** menu.

3. Now select the **Measure** menu and the **Distance** command.

4. Select each endpoint of the line.

AutoSketch will tell you the distance between points in the dialogue box that appears. An example appears below.

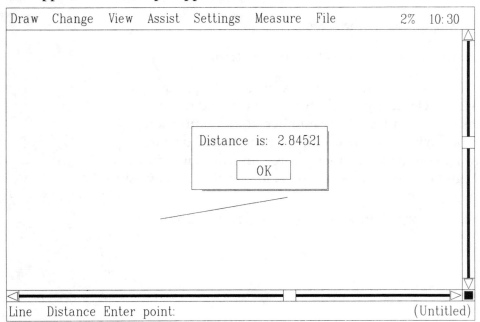

The Angle Command

Besides measuring distances between points, AutoSketch can also measure the number of degrees in angles. Look at the illustration and follow the steps below to measure angles between two bearings (directions).

AutoSketch®
Reference
Manual
pp. 3 - 4

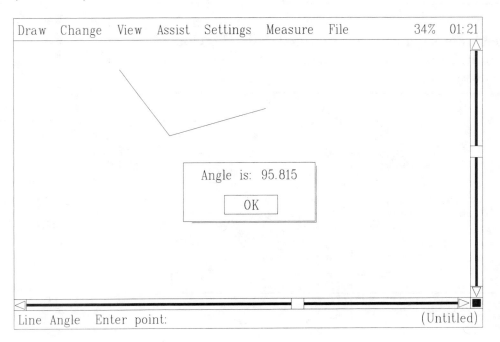

1. Draw two intersecting lines as shown.

2. Select the **Angle** command.

3. Pick a base point.

This point is the intersection of the two lines forming the angle that you want to measure.

4. Then pick a point for the first direction.

This location tells AutoSketch where to start measuring the angle.

5. Last, pick a point for the second direction.

By picking direction points, you tell AutoSketch to measure the angle in either a clockwise or a counterclockwise direction. A dialogue box will appear with the measurement of the angle in degrees.

The Bearing Command

*AutoSketch®
Reference
Manual*
pp.17 - 18

What if you want to measure the angle of direction between objects in a drawing? You can use the Bearing command to calculate the bearing from the first point to the second point.

▶ *Hint:*

In AutoSketch measurements, 0° is located at the 3 o'clock position (on the X-axis). Measurements are made in a counterclockwise direction.

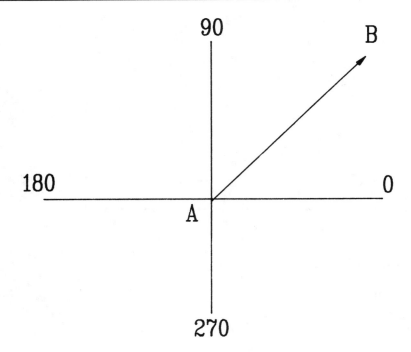

Let's measure some bearing angles.

1.   Select the **Bearing** command.

2.   Pick a base point location.

This point is the starting point for a rubberband line forming an angle from the X-axis.

3.   Move the rubberband line around and note the measurement as it changes in the prompt area.

4.   Pick a point.

A dialogue box like the one on the next page will appear with the number of degrees in the bearing angle.

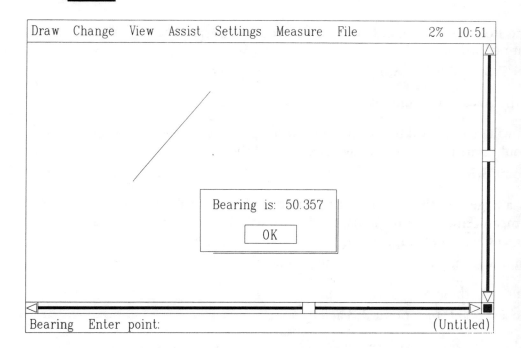

AutoSketch®
Reference
Manual

The Area Command

AutoSketch figures the area inside an object and the *perimeter* (distance around the object) when you use the Area command. When it calculates the perimeter, it remembers all the points you select and assumes that there are straight lines between them. To practice using this command, use the illustration and the steps that follow.

pp. 7 - 8

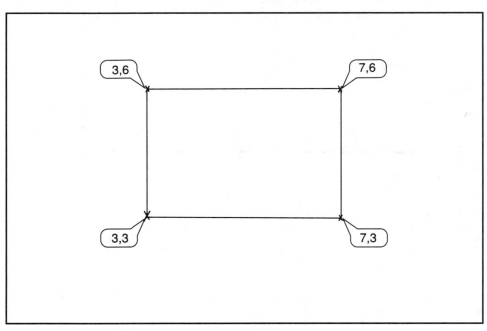

1. Use the **Polyline** command and draw a rectangle, using the following absolute coordinates:

   3,3   7,3   7,6   3,6   3,3

2. Select the **Area** command.

AutoSketch will prompt you to pick a point on the perimeter (outside) of the object where it should start measuring the distance around the object.

3. Pick point **3,3.**

You will see a large X at that point. AutoSketch uses this X to show you where you started the measurement. You will have to return to this starting point to tell AutoSketch to start calculating.

4. Continue selecting points around the perimeter.

AutoSketch marks these points with small Xs.

5. For the last point, pick point **3,3** again.

A dialogue box will appear with two measurements: the area inside the rectangle and the distance between the perimeter points you picked.

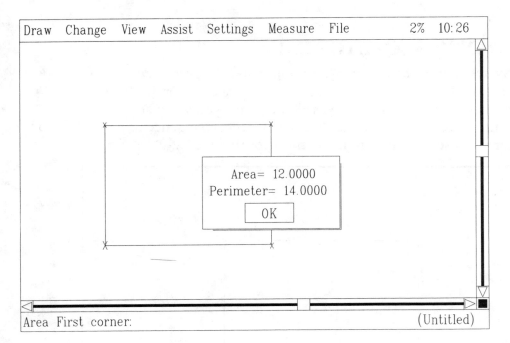

The Angle Dimension Command

AutoSketch®
Reference
Manual
p. 4
pp. 56 - 65

The next four commands on the Measure menu are used to calculate *dimensions* in drawings. Dimensions are exact measurements of lines, angles, and radii that are marked on drawings. AutoSketch shows them in the same way you would on a paper drawing. It draws

■ *extension lines* showing what distance is being measured

■ *dimension lines* between extension lines (these lines have arrowheads on both ends).

You can tell AutoSketch to draw in the dimension either above or below the dimension line. It "writes" the measurement in the style you have set up using the Text command on the Settings menu.

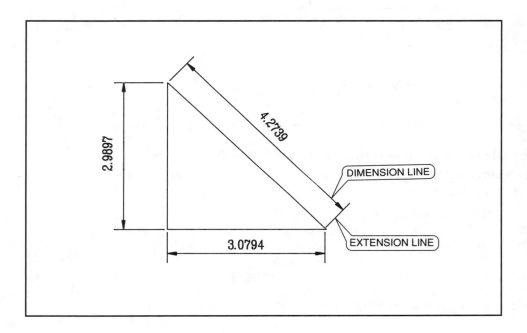

The Angle Dimension command calculates an angle between two lines and places the measurement and dimension line, or arc, on the drawing. The lines can be intersecting or nonintersecting. To try this

command, follow the directions below.

1. Pick the **Draw** menu and the **Polyline** command.

2. Draw lines like the ones below.

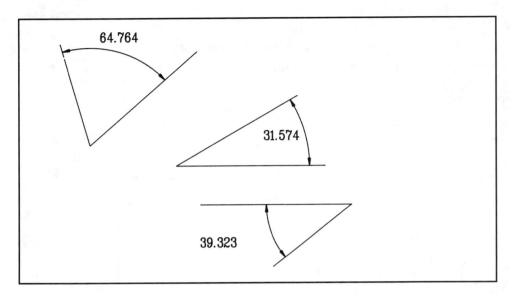

3. Pick the **Measure** menu and the **Angle Dimension** command. AutoSketch prompts you to select the first line and then the second line for measuring the angle.

4. Choose a pair of lines that you have drawn and pick one of them.

5. Pick the second line.

6. Select a point for the dimension line and measurement.

7. Place dimensions on the remaining angles on your drawing.

Dimension Arrow

pp. 63 - 64

You can change the style of dimension arrow that is drawn with the Arrow command on the Settings menu. You can also change an existing dimension by applying a new style with the Change menu.

1. Select the **Arrow** command on the **Settings** menu.

A dialogue box appears showing the different styles to choose from.

2. Choose a new style and close the dialogue box.

Now apply the new style to a dimension you drew in the last section. (If you want to make sure that you apply only the arrow change, you can select the Property command on the Settings menu and turn the other properties off.)

3. Select the **Property** command on the **Change** menu.

4. Select the dimension you want to change.

The new dimension will appear.

The Align Dimension Command

AutoSketch®
Reference
Manual
p. 3
pp. 56 - 65

The Align Dimension command places the dimensions lines and measurements parallel to the lines being measured. Each dimension is aligned (lined up) between two points. The points can be at any angle and distance apart. Let's see how these measurements look.

1. Use the **Polyline** command to draw a shape similar to the one below.

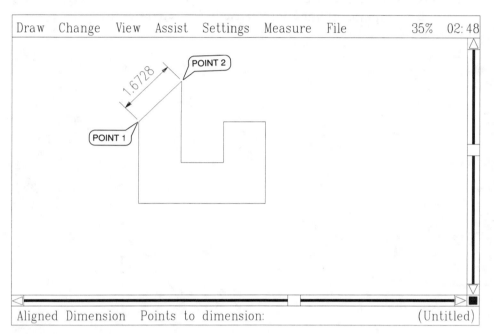

2. Select the **Align Dimension** command.

"Aligned dimension Points to dimension:" appears in the prompt area.

3. Select a point similar to point 1 in the illustration.

This point is the starting point of the dimension line. Usually it is the corner of the object that you are going to measure.

4. Now pick a point similar to point 2 in the illustration.

This point is the endpoint of the dimension line. The dimension line tells AutoSketch the distance to be measured. Now you need to tell AutoSketch where to put the measurement on the drawing.

5. Pick a point close to the center of the line being measured and slightly above it.

What happens on the screen? AutoSketch should have automatically inserted the dimension line with an arrowhead at each end, parallel to the measured line and passing through the third point you selected. The exact measurement between the first two points you selected should be placed above the dimension line. An aligned dimension is always positioned on the drawing at the angle you choose when you select the dimension points.

The Horizontal Dimension Command

Unit 11

AutoSketch® Reference Manual
pp. 56 - 65
p. 100

The Horizontal Dimension command works like the Align Dimension command except that you can only use it to measure horizontal distance between two points. In an object like the one below, you can see how AutoSketch measured only the straight distances across the object. This feature is helpful when you need to dimension an object with many different horizontal levels. Since angles are not considered in the measurement, you can place dimension lines with arrowheads where you want them in a short time.

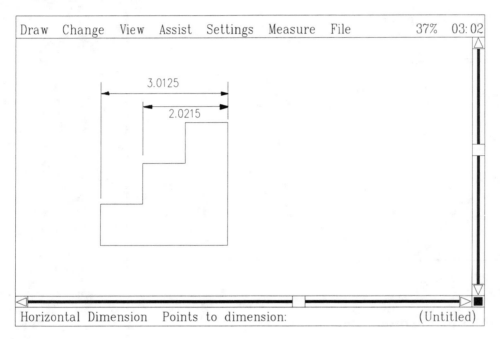

| Draw   Change   View   Assist   Settings   Measure   File   37%   03:02 |

3.0125

2.0215

Horizontal Dimension   Points to dimension: (Untitled)

Exercise 1

Create a shape like the one in the illustration above and dimension its top line. Try placing the measurement below the dimension line. Select a new dimension arrow and a new type of text for the dimension line.

The Vertical Dimension Command

*AutoSketch®
Reference
Manual*

**pp. 56 - 65
p. 214**

The Vertical Dimension command measures only vertical distance between two points. For the shape below, AutoSketch has calculated only the vertical dimensions. You can place the text on either the right side or the left side of the dimension line.

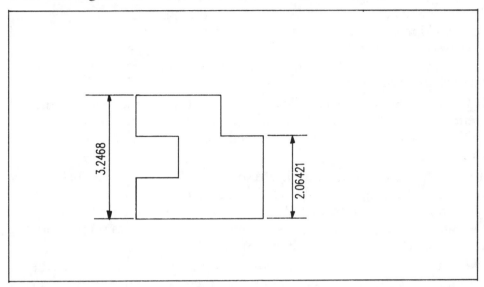

✔✔ *Exercise 2*

Create a shape like the one above and dimension the vertical lines.

Stretching Dimensions

AutoSketch treats dimensions like single objects. If you stretch a dimensioned object so that the measurements change, AutoSketch will automatically remeasure the object and draw the new dimensions.

p. 64

Key Terms

perimeter
dimensions

extension lines
dimension lines

My Dream

by Jeff Walker

I had a dream one day. It was very scary. This is how it went. My friend Chad and I were talking about the weird things that have been happening very often. Kids were getting kidnapped all over town. We thought we might like to get to the bottom of this mystery. We thought we would do a little investigating.

We decided to leave the next morning. We figured a good place to look for the people that had been kidnapping all the kids would be way back in the woods at the Old Crackling Mansion. Chad and I traveled for many days. After a week went by we had finally made it to the Mansion. Chad suggested we go to sleep and start investigating first thing in the morning.

The following morning we climbed an old tree that had broken and fallen on the roof, and we went in the window of the Old Crackling Mansion. After we had reached the attic door we heard noises, so we opened the door and saw a lot of kids that had been kidnapped.

We started to walk forward, but then we heard footsteps. We ran and hid behind an old cabinet. We saw an ugly guy walk by. He had big horns growing from his face. After the guy walked by we started to walk downstairs, but as we were walking down the stairs another similar looking creature was walking up and there was no place for us to go because that other guy was coming down.

We were locked in a room where it was air tight. There was only one bed and one window. Then I figured I could break the window, but there was only one way to do it, and that was to jump through it. I figured Chad was willing to jump through it, but he said no, so that left me.

I ran and jumped off the bed and dove through the window. Then Chad was in a hurry to get out, so he jumped out and landed right on top of me. We walked out and saw a lot of ugly creatures guarding little kids that were eating. One of the kids said, "We could all get out of here and escape if we only could get the key."

We had to take the keys that were in the pocket of the leader's pants. The leader looked as if it was part girl and part boy. We had to unlock the gate out front, so we had to go through the attic and wait until she was asleep.

We waited for an hour, and she finally fell asleep. We managed to get the keys, but at the last second she woke up. We jumped through the window. Since she was pretty big, we never thought she could follow us out the window. I don't know how she did it, but when we got out, she was waiting there for us!

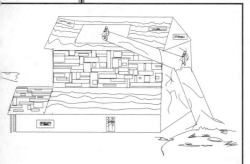

We finally managed to get away by doing some good moves on her, and we got to the gate. I unlocked the gate, and she was turning very very ugly. She was turning green. She had a brain-like substance growing on her face until she exploded, and we were safe for the time being. After all the evil creatures were gone, we were free to lead the kids to safety.

Jeff Walker was a reluctant writer before his teacher, Grace Vento-Zogby, encouraged him to write this story and illustrate it with AutoSketch. He began with an idea, then drew the picture. The illustration sparked his interest in completing the story. At the time, he was a sixth grade student at Sauquoit Valley Central School, Sauquoit, New York.

Let's Review

Questions

1. How can you find the coordinates of a point in a drawing?

   _____

   _____

2. What information can you discover by using the Show Properties command?

   _____

   _____

3. How can you measure the distance between two points in a drawing when you don't want to place the measurement on the drawing?

   _____

   _____

4. What three points do you select when you use the Angle command to measure an angle?

   _____

   _____

5. Where does AutoSketch locate 0° when it measures bearing, and in what direction from this location does it measure?

   _____

   _____

6. What two measurements are made with the Area command?

   _____

   _____

7. What information do you have to enter for AutoSketch to draw in an aligned dimension?

   _____

   _____

8. How do the Horizontal Dimension and Vertical Dimension commands limit what you can measure in a drawing?

_____

_____

9. What happens to dimensions when you stretch an object?

_____

Extend Your Knowledge

1. On graph paper, draw polygons like the ones below. Count each square on the graph paper as one unit. In units, measure the perimeter of (distance around) each polygon.

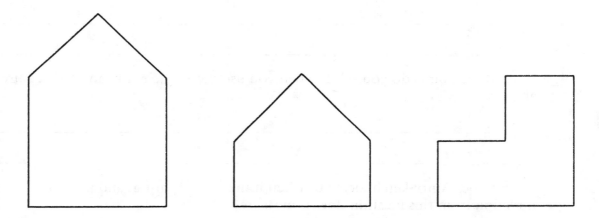

2. Use the drawing you made in problem 1. Use a protractor to measure the angles inside each of the polygons. Add the dimensions, or measurements, to the drawing.

3. Once again, use the drawing you made in problem 1. Measure the horizontal and vertical dimensions of each polygon. Add the dimensions to your drawing.

UNIT 12

The File Menu

Objectives:

■ *To review how to begin new drawings, save drawings, find drawings you have saved, and end a drawing session.*

■ *To print or plot drawings.*

■ *To create drawing files that can be used with other CAD software.*

■ *To learn how to make and view drawing slides.*

■ *To play the Tick-Tack-Toe game with the computer.*

AutoSketch®
Reference
Manual

pp. 80 - 81

The File menu contains the "odds and ends" of the AutoSketch software, but these features make AutoSketch practical and useful.

Draw	Change	View	Assist	Settings	Measure	File		29%	12:00

```
                                        New
                                        Open
                                        Part Clip
                                        Save
                                        Save As

                                        Pen Info
                                        PlotArea
                                        Plot Name
                                        Plot

                                        Make DXF
                                        Read DXF
                                        Make Macro
                                        Read Macro
                                        Make Slide
                                        View Slide

                                        Information
                                        Game
                                        Quit
```

(Untitled)

You can make files to use with AutoCAD and other CAD programs, make hard copies of your drawings, and even play a game to see if you can outsmart the computer.

Unit
12

AutoSketch®
Reference
Manual

pp. 67 - 69
p. 118

The New Command

You have already used the New command many times as you have made drawings with AutoSketch. When you select this command, you are telling AutoSketch to start another drawing. With this option, you can get a clean drawing area with "(Untitled)" in the corner without having to exit the program and reload it into the computer's memory. Remember that when you use the New command, you will see a dialogue box that reminds you to either save the drawing you are working on, discard it, or cancel the New command.

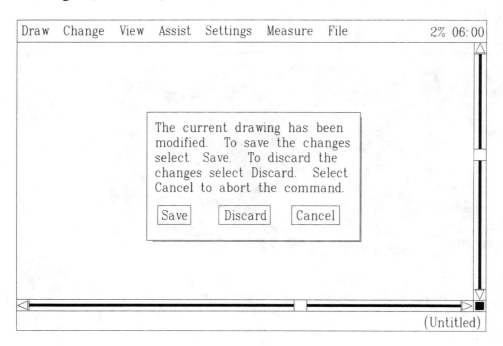

Draw   Change   View   Assist   Settings   Measure   File   2% 06:00

The current drawing has been modified. To save the changes select Save. To discard the changes select Discard. Select Cancel to abort the command.

Save   Discard   Cancel

(Untitled)

The Open Command

*AutoSketch®
Reference
Manual*
**pp. 67 - 69
p. 119**

The Open command lets you choose a drawing you have previously created and saved. You already know how to move through the list in the dialogue box to find the drawing you want.

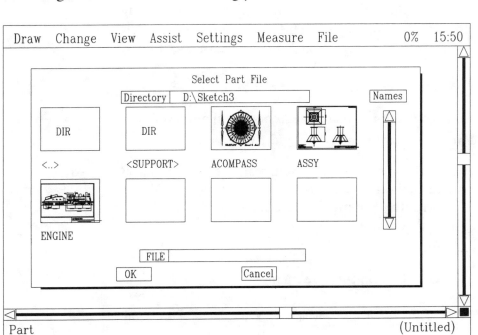

But what if the drawing you are looking for isn't there? Maybe you have stored it on another disk or in another subdirectory. In that case, you can use the Directory box to find it.

1.   Select **Open** under the **File** menu.

When you first use the Open command, this box shows the directory of the disk you are currently using. If you tell AutoSketch to look in another directory, it will give you another list of drawing files.

2.   Move the arrow to the box next to **Directory**.

3.   Type the subdirectory name or the drive label.

For example, the drawings files might be on the C drive in a subdirectory called SKETCH3\DWGFILES. For this example, you would type the following: C:\ SKETCH3\DWGFILES. See Appendix A for information on directories and subdirectories.

4.   Select the **Ok** box.

You should now see the files listed.

The Part Clip Command

AutoSketch®
Reference
Manual
pp. 125 -
129

The Part Clip command is like the Part command on the Draw menu. The difference is that the Part Clip command can take segments (parts) from a drawing and record them in another drawing file. The idea is to save parts that you like and use them in new drawings without having to redraw the details over again and again. This can be a real time saver! This command works with the Part Base command on the Settings menu.

1.   Create two or more objects on a new drawing.

For example, you might want to create a skateboard on a sidewalk.

2.   Select the **Part Base** command on the **Settings** menu.

The Part Insertion Base Point dialogue box appears. The Part Clip Base Point box is already turned on because it is the default setting. When you create a part file with the File menu, AutoSketch will ask for a part insertion base because this option is on.

3.   Close the dialogue box.

4.   Select the **Part Clip** box on the **File** menu

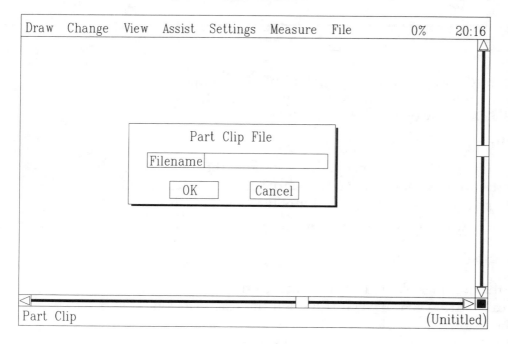

5.   Type in a name for the new part clip and close the dialogue box.

6.   Pick a point near an object that you would like to make into a part file.

7.   Select the object.

The object will be highlighted. You can get out of this mode by selecting another command.

8. Select the **New** command on the **File** menu. (Save the original drawing.)

9. Select the **Part** command on the **Draw** menu.

10. Find and select the part you just created.

11. Insert the part into the new drawing.

12. Finish a drawing that includes the inserted part.

The Save Command

You have already learned that you must use the Save command to store a finished drawing. But it has another important use. It is wise to use the Save command while you are drawing. Someone may accidentally unplug the computer, and your drawing would disappear. Or computer signals may get scrambled so that you need to turn the computer off and then on again in order to keep working. Or you may leave your workstation and come back to find someone else working there. A good rule to follow for saving your work is to use the Save command every 15 minutes. If you do, you can only lose 15 minutes of your hard work.

The Save dialogue box gives you the option of storing your drawing files on a disk drive other than the one you are using.

To do this, type the name of the drive and file in the File Name box. For example, you could type in C:\SKETCH3\project 1 or A:project2.

AutoSketch®
Reference
Manual

pp. 176 -
177

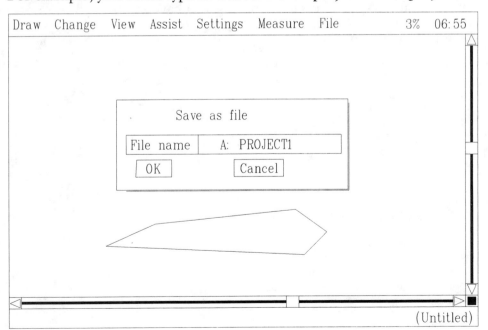

The Save As Command

So far you have used the Save As command to save a new drawing. But you can also use it to change the name of a drawing you are looking at. By saving the same drawing under different names, you can keep several copies of it. You can even do this as you are adding elements to it or editing it to keep several versions. These copies would show how you developed the completed drawing. The Save As commands bring up the same dialogue box as the Save command.

The Make DXF™ Command

The Make DXF command gives you the option to transfer an AutoSketch drawing into another form that can be used with AutoCAD software. DXF stands for "drawing exchange format." With the DXF process, your drawing can be used with AutoCAD version 2.5 or higher software. You can also use a DXF file in all major word processing or desktop publishing programs.

▶ *Hint:*

You can distinguish between an AutoSketch drawing file and a DXF drawing file by the DOS extension used. AutoSketch uses SKD for the extension. A DXF file uses DXF. You can read more about file extensions in Appendix A.

Let's try the process and make a DXF file out of a drawing file.

1. Load AutoSketch.

2. Use the **Open** command to get access to a drawing you have saved.

3. Select the **Make DXF** command.

AutoSketch®
Reference
Manual
p. 177

pp. 70 - 71
p. 112

A dialogue box will be shown on the screen asking you to select the name of the new DXF file. You can either enter a new name or select the name you gave the drawing when you saved it.

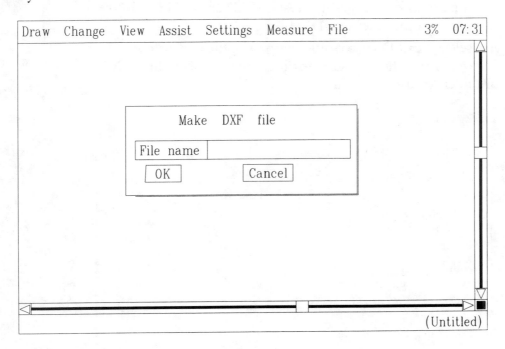

4. Close the dialogue box by picking **OK**.

The file is now ready to pull into AutoCAD software. The AutoCAD main menu has a DXF IN command that you would use to transfer the file. You would type in the drive label (like C:, for example), a backslash (\), the subdirectory and another backslash (if you were using this division), and the DXF file name. After you pressed the Enter key, you could use AutoCAD software to make further changes in the drawing you created using AutoSketch.

The Read DXF Command

The Read DXF command reads in a DXF file to your computer and screen. This command inputs files from AutoCAD and other software programs that have output files in a DXF format.

When you select Read DXF, a dialogue box like the one below appears on the screen. The dialogue box lists the DXF files currently in the drive or directory you are using.

AutoSketch® Reference Manual pp. 70 - 71 p. 167

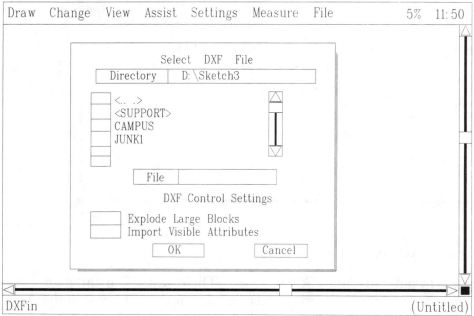

The Pen Info Command

With the Pen Info command, you begin the process of plotting your drawing. If you have a graphics printer, you can use this command to set the printing speed. You will see a dialogue box like the one in the following illustration.

p. 141 pp. 145 - 155

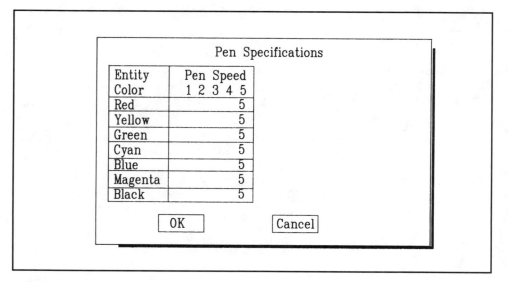

If you are using a pen plotter, you can use this command to select both the pens to be used and the speed of each one.

	Pen Specifications	
Entity Color	Pen Number 1 2 3 4 5 6	Pen Speed 1 2 3 4 5
Red	1	5
Yellow	1	5
Green	1	5
Cyan	1	5
Blue	1	5
Magenta	1	5
Black	1	5

OK   Cancel

The Pen Specifications dialogue box has sections for selecting pens. The left section shows you the locations of the pens in the plotter indexing carousel. This device holds the pens in the plotter so they can be indexed to the plotter pen grappler (the device that moves the pens). To check the location of the pens, check your plotter carousel to make sure that the pen position numbers are the same as those shown in the dialogue box.

The section on the right shows the choices you have for plotter speed. How do you know what speed to choose? That depends upon different factors, such as the type of plotter you have or the type of pen used. Some plotters have speeds that are adjustable, where 1 is the slowest speed and 5 is the fastest. A complicated drawing may plot best at a slower speed. Also, if you want high quality when plotting, use a slower speed.

If your plotter is not adjustable, it might use a default value for the speed. In other words, the plotter will run at one speed no matter what you choose.

Let's start setting up a plotting process.

1. Use the **Open** command to get the drawing from Unit 10, problem 1, on your screen.

You may need to go back to problem 1 in Unit 10 to create the drawing now.

2. Select the **Pen Info** command.

If your plotter uses a carousel, the dialogue box shows choices for pen number and pen speed. Go to step 7.

If your plotter uses only one pen, the dialogue box shows choices for pen speed only. Follow the steps below.

3. Move the arrow pointer so that it lines up next to the **Red** box.

4. Select the number of the pen speed you want to use when plotting the color red.

5. Assign a pen speed to the color yellow, and so on, until a speed is selected for each color.

6. Close the dialogue box.

If your plotter has a carousel, follow the steps below.

7. Move the arrow pointer so that it lines up next to the **Red** box.

8. Select the pen number that corresponds with the number on the carousel for red.

9. Move the arrow pointer to the section on the right and select the speed you want to use when plotting the color red.

10. Assign a pen number and speed to the color yellow, and so on, until all the colors are set up.

Do you think it is necessary to indicate a pen location in the dialogue box if you are not plotting with that color? No— entering a pen location on the screen won't make any difference in actual plotting.

You can also use colors for varying pen tip thicknesses. Just use the colors to stand for the different thicknesses.

Remember, you must use the Pen Information command to set colors and speeds each time you plot a drawing.

The Print/Plot Area Command

After you use the Pen Information command to select pen colors and speeds, use the Print/Plot Area command to continue preparing to print or plot your drawing. If your computer is configured for a printer, the command will say Print Area. If it is configured for a plotter, it will say Plot Area. Follow the dialogue box below and the steps to enter the necessary information.

pp. 144 - 155

```
Draw   Change   View   Assist   Settings   Measure   File          3%    07:31

                          Paper   Size
               A (11 X 8.5 in.)        A4 (297 X 210 mm)
               Inches                  Millimeters

                       Plot   Box   Settings
               Create Plot Box        X  Plot Size   7.83333
               Create Clip Box        Y  Plot Size   10.5

               Plot to Extents        Rotate 90 Degrees

                          Scaling
                  Drawing Units   Plotting Units
                        1            =  1
                         OK              Cancel


                                                           (Untitled)
```

1. Bring up the **Print/Plot Area** dialogue box.

In the boxes under Paper size you see the standard sizes of sheets that your printer or plotter can use. The number of choices you see depends upon the type of plotter or printer chosen when AutoSketch was configured, or set up. The Plot Area dialogue box shown on the previous page is for a printer.

The sizes shown give the length and width of the paper, as well as the letter that identifies the size of paper it is. The letter designation is useful information for engineers, drafters, typesetters, and so on. The possible sizes range from A = 11 x 8 1/2 inches to E = 36 x 48 inches.

A check mark is shown in either the "Inches" or "Millimeters" box to indicate which measurement is used for the standard sizes.

2. Highlight the box next to the A paper size and press your pick button.

A check mark will appear in this box and the Inches box. (These may already be checked by default.)

▶ *Hint:*

> You can also enter any other size of paper that will work on your hardware by typing values in the X Plot Size and Y Plot Size boxes and toggling on either Inches or Millimeters. But be sure that these values aren't greater than the measurements of the largest standard paper size. AutoSketch will display a warning message if values are too large.

3. Next, enter **2** in the **Drawing Units** box and 1 in the **Plotting Units** box.

Values in these two boxes determine how the drawing on your screen will compare in size to the drawing printed or plotted on paper. You have set up a 2 to 1 plot scale. The size in drawing units on your screen is twice as big as the plotted drawing will be. If you enter 4 Drawing Units = 1 Plotting Unit, the hard copy of the drawing will be one-quarter the size of the screen drawing.

▶ *Hint:*

> This scale works even if you have reduced the size of your screen drawing by using the Zoom commands. AutoSketch uses drawing units to determine the scale. The way the units are currently shown on your screen doesn't matter in setting up the plot scale.

4. Turn the **Rotate by 90 degrees** box **On**.

The rotate feature is useful for fitting more images on the paper..

5. Leave the **Create Plot Box** feature turned **On**.

The *plot box* is a rectangle that shows you what part of your drawing will fit on the paper when you print or plot. It doesn't appear in the plotted drawing, but it becomes a part of the screen drawing if you save the file. You can plot a drawing even if you don't tell AutoSketch to create a plot box. But seeing it on the screen will help you know just what part of the drawing will be plotted.

```
Plot box 1 — 10.5 X 9.74
```

6. Close the dialogue box and select the Accept box.

AutoSketch places the lower left corner of the plot box in the lower left corner of the screen. The location of the upper right corner depends on the paper size, plot scale, and rotation used. You can make several plot boxes for a drawing, but only one can be visible when you plot.

Check to see if a plot box appears. If you can't see the plot box, follow this step.

7. Go to the **View** menu and select the **Last Plot Box** command.

p. 101
pp. 144 - 145

The Last Plot Box command fills the screen with the last plot box you created.

You can change the plot box after AutoSketch draws it on the screen by using Edit commands like Move, Erase, and Scale. That is, you can change the location of the plot box, remove it, or reduce or increase its size. If you make it larger, the drawing elements within it will be plotted smaller, since more of the drawing will have to fit on the same sheet of paper. If you shrink the plot box, the drawing elements are larger on the hard copy.

If you erase the plot box, you can go back to the Plot Area command and change its size by entering a different value for drawing units. If the plot box was too small, enter a larger value. For example, use 1.5 instead of 1. If the plot box was too large, enter a smaller number. For example, use .75 instead of 1. Then compare the size of the plot box and the drawing again.

8.   Adjust the plot box until it includes as much of the drawing as you want to plot.

You can also use the Plot Area command to create a *clip box*. A clip box is a smaller section of the plot box. If you have created a clip box on a drawing, only the elements within the clip box will be plotted. You would use this feature if you wanted to zero in on a certain detail within a plot box. You can use the Edit commands to change a clip box as well as a plot box.

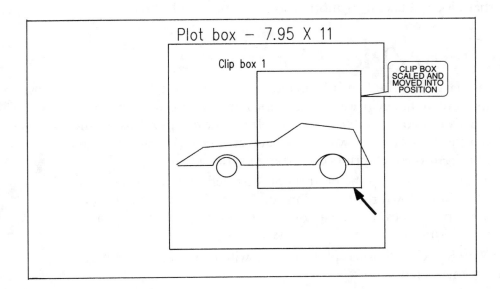

There is also a box called Plot to Extents. If this box is checked, the entire drawing is automatically placed in a plot box. AutoSketch sets the scale factor so that everything will fit. You may want to rotate the drawing to better fit the type of paper you are using.

The Print/Plot Name Command

You can use the Print/Plot Name command only if you have selected this option when you set up your system. See the *AutoSketch Installation and Performance Guide*, pp. 53 - 54. If your system is set up to use this command, you can enter a file name in a Plot File Name dialogue box. AutoSketch will then hold the information it needs to plot the drawing in a plot file and keep the computer open and available for more drawing work. At the end of a drawing session, all of the drawings you want to plot can be processed at one time. If you tell AutoSketch to create the plot file on a separate disk, you can even remove that disk and take it to another workstation for plotting.

*AutoSketch®
Reference
Manual*
pp. 145 -
155

The Print/Plot Command

After you have used the Pen Information and Print/Plot Area commands, you are finally ready to start plotting. The Print/Plot command activates your printer or plotter. If you have a plot box on the screen, your plotter or printer will plot whatever appears within. If there is no plot box, AutoSketch prints everything in the drawing.

pp. 144 -
155

What if you want to stop the plotting process before your hard copy is finished? Just hold down the Ctrl (Control) key and strike the letter C key. After the portion of the drawing that is stored in the memory of the printer or plotter is drawn, the process will stop.

When AutoSketch is finished plotting, you will see the arrow pointer reappear on the screen.

The Make and Read Macro Commands

Macros are programs that record a series of actions that you want AutoSketch to perform by itself. You can use them to make a record of things you do over and over. After you create and record a macro with the Assist menu, you can store it in a text file with the Make Macro command on the File menu. The macro commands will be stored in a file with an .MCR extension. You can then use the Read Macro command to read the file. These commands are not necessary to run macros, but you might want to use them when making changes to the macros. For example, you could make changes to a stored macro with a word processor.

The Make Slide Command

*AutoSketch®
Reference
Manual*
**p. 113
pp. 183 -
185**

The Make slide command converts an existing drawing into an easily-viewed *computer slide*. The term "slide" may give you the idea that you are creating a slide similar to that produced by a 35 mm or 110 camera. The type of slide you are producing recreates an existing AutoSketch drawing, but faster. In other words, you can bring up an AutoSketch slide in about two-thirds the time it would normally take to generate your regular drawing.

To create a computer-generated slide, all you need is a drawing created with AutoSketch.

1. Create and save a drawing, or open a file with a drawing you have saved.

2. Select the **Make Slide** command.

A dialogue box appears. The name of the drawing should appear in the File name box.

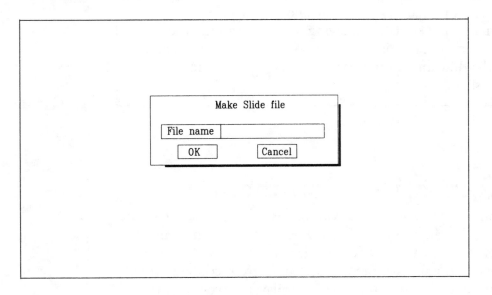

3. Select **OK** to accept the name that appears in the box.

Your software converts the contents of the file. You now have two files that are separate from each other.

A drawing file has a DOS extension .SKD, and AutoSketch gives the new slide file the DOS extension .SLD. For example, a drawing file named AIRPLANE.SKD becomes AIRPLANE.SLD.

The View Slide Command

After you make a slide, use the View Slide command to bring it to the screen. Slide viewing quickly turns computer generated images into visual images. They are often used for viewing business charts and building plans, or to enhance speeches with computer enhanced graphics.

1. Select the **File** menu and the **View Slide** command.

You will see a directory that shows the files located within it. You can select one of the files listed or change directories.

2. Select a slide file.

You should now see the slide produced on the screen.

AutoSketch®
Reference
Manual
pp. 183 -
185
p. 215

▶ *Hint:*

> Once a slide has been made, you cannot alter or add drawing elements to it. Any changes you make and save while viewing a slide are actually applied to the drawing file, even though they appear to be part of the slide file. To make changes to a slide file, go back to the drawing file and use the Make Slide command to create a new slide.

The Information Command

The File menu contains some extra commands that don't relate to the process of making drawings. One of these is the Information command. By using this command, you can find out the version of the AutoSketch software in your computer. You can also see the current configuration. This includes information about the type of display, the type of printer or plotter, and the input device.

p. 100

The Game Command

AutoSketch®
Reference
Manual
p. 96

For a change of pace on a slow drawing day, AutoSketch lets you play a unique Tick-Tack-Toe game against the computer by using the Game command. To find out how to play, select Help in the dialogue box. When you no longer want to play, close the dialogue box and return to drawing. So far, the authors haven't beaten the computer at the game, but some of our games finished in ties. Maybe your luck will be better than ours.

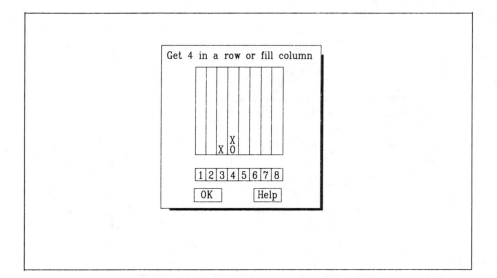

The Quit Command

As you already know, the Quit command lets you end a drawing session. Selecting it brings up a dialogue box on your screen (unless you didn't draw anything after you loaded AutoSketch). This box lets you save what you have drawn, throw it away, or change your mind about quitting. Once you have activated the Quit command, you have ended your session with AutoSketch.

AutoSketch®
Reference
Manual
p. 166

| Draw | Change | View | Assist | Settings | Measure | File | 2% 06:00 |

The current drawing has been modified. To save the changes select Save. To discard the changes select Discard. Select Cancel to abort the command.

Save   Discard   Cancel

(Untitled)

Key Terms

plot box   clip box   computer slide

Let's Review

Questions

1. When you are pulling a drawing out of the file using the Open command, how can you tell AutoSketch to look in a different directory?

    _____

    _____

2. How often should you use the Save command during a drawing session?

    _____

3. Why is the Save As command useful?

    _____

    _____

4. What AutoSketch command is used to create drawing exchange format files?

    _____

5. Name the two kinds of information that you give AutoSketch using the Pen Information command.

    _____

    _____

6. What is a part clip?

    _____

    _____

7. What three commands do you use to make a hard copy of a drawing?

    _____

    _____

Problems

1. Open up one of your drawings and plot it at a scale of .5 drawing units = 1 plotting unit. Then plot it with a new plot box and a scale of .25 drawing units = 1 plotting unit. Next, plot it with the Plot to Extents box turned on. Finally, create a clip box around a portion of the drawing and plot it. Compare the results of the plots.

2. You have been hired by a sporting goods manufacturer to design a new skateboard. Draw several models with different patterns the manufacturer may choose from. Make slides for each drawing. Ask a group of your classmates to act as the manufacturer and present your slides to them.

Extend Your Knowledge

1. Find three or four 35mm or comparable slides. You may have some at home. Mount the slides on a sheet of paper or cardboard and write a description of each one. Now write a comparison of how slides are shown in a projector and how the View Slide option works in AutoSketch.

2. Make a list of all the drawings you have completed to date while using this workbook. Next to each drawing, note the disk or directory where the drawing is located.

3. Use the Text command to create letters about 4" high. Print or plot the letters and use them to construct your school name in a 3' to 4' banner.

1. Follow the dimensions shown to draw the following figure. Do not add the dimensions to your drawing.

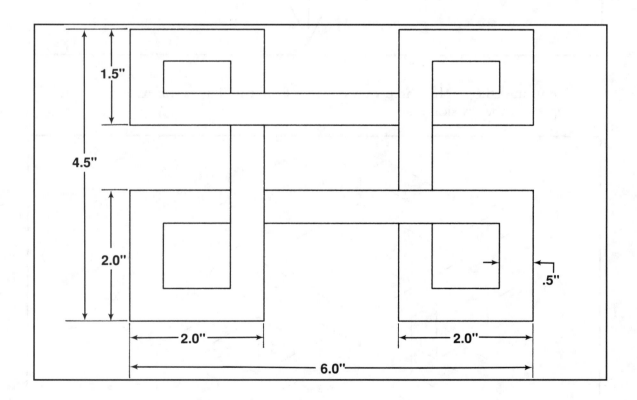

2. Draw the following figure. First, form a diamond with a height of 2 inches and a width of 1 inch. Then, create a circular array around the bottom point of the diamond.

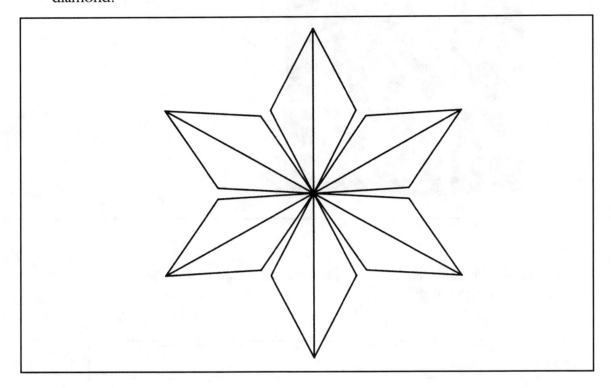

3. Draw an orthographic three-view drawing from this illustration. Use .5 inch to represent the division marks.

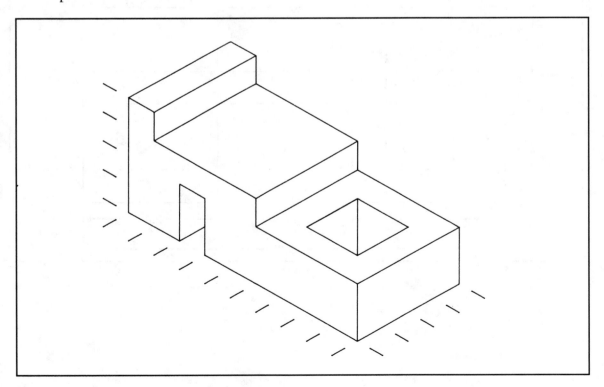

4.   Draw an orthographic three-view drawing from this illustration. Use .5 inch to represent the division marks.

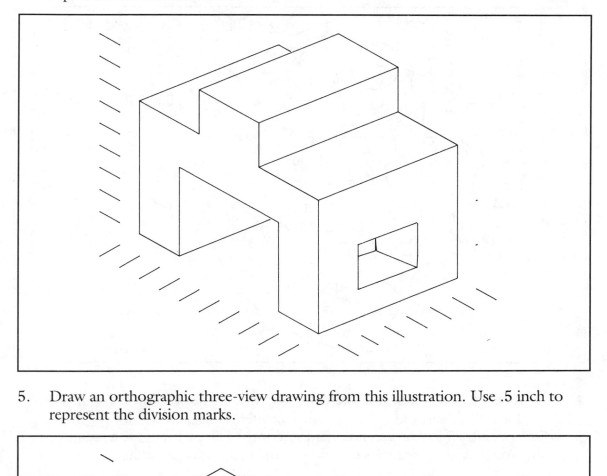

5.   Draw an orthographic three-view drawing from this illustration. Use .5 inch to represent the division marks.

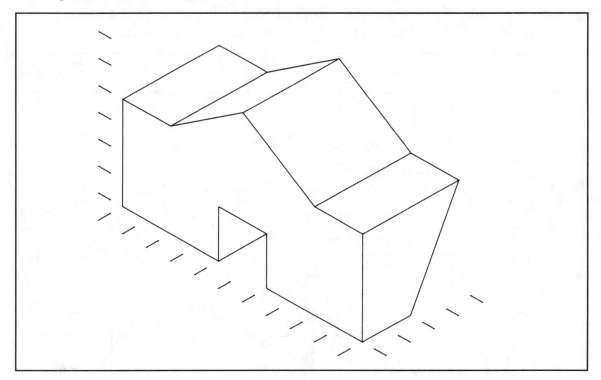

6. Use the dimensions shown to draw the following figure.

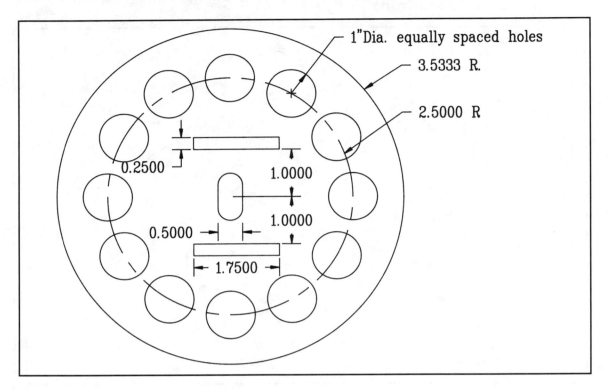

7. Use the dimensions shown to draw the following figure. Use these commands: Arc, Line, Chamfer, and Fillet. For the Chamfer setting, use 1.5 for the first distance and .75 for the second distance. For the Fillet setting, use a radius of 1 unit. You may also want to use a grid and snap setting of .25 units.

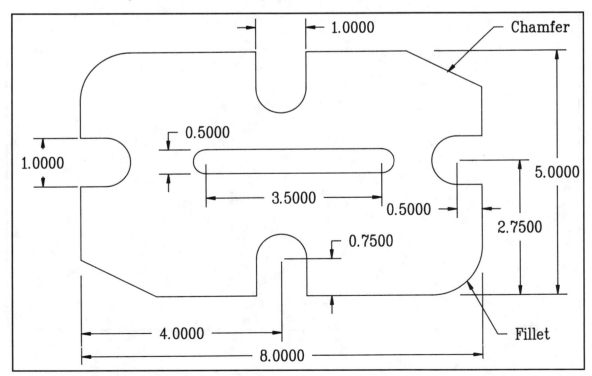

8. Draw an isometric or oblique drawing from this illustration. To make the drawing fit on the screen area, use .5 inch or .25 inch to represent division marks. For extra practice, use this illustration to create a full, half, or quarter section drawing. Include cross hatching and dimensioning.

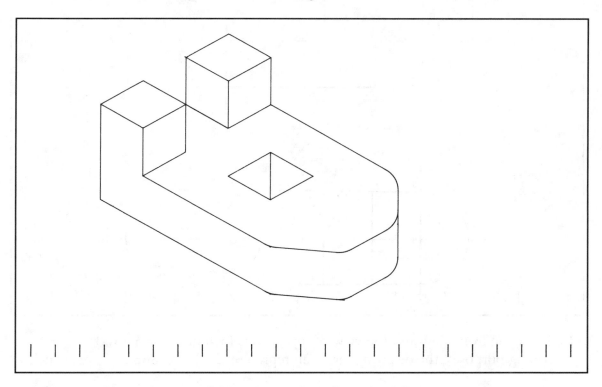

9. Follow the directions in problem 8.

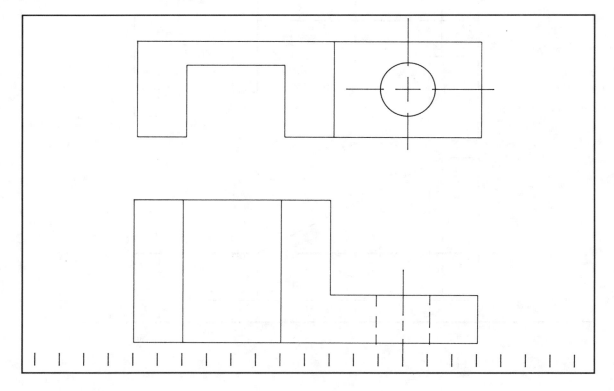

10. Follow the directions in problem 8.

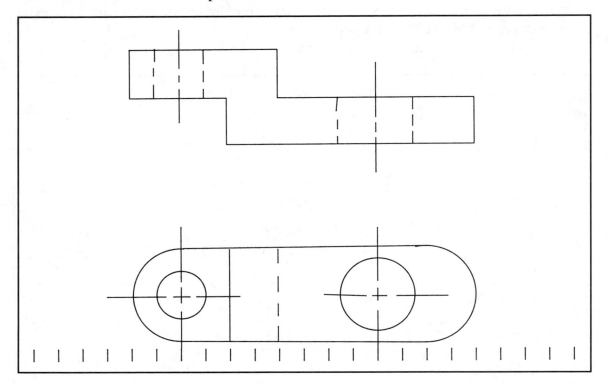

11. Draw the front view and top view of this object. Include the dimensions. For scaling purposes, the division marks can represent .25 inch, .385 inch, or .5 inch.

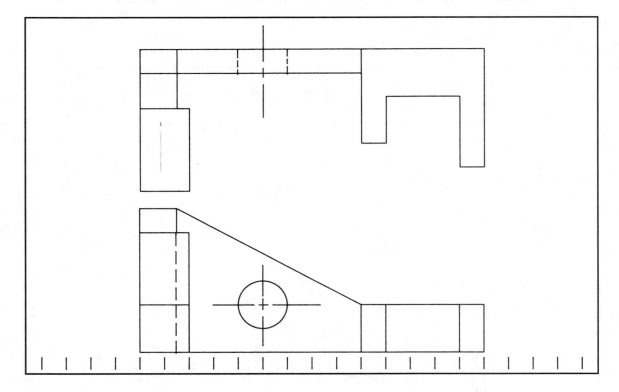

12. Draw the object below and add dimensions. Also, try an oblique or isometric drawing. The division marks can be .25 inch or .5 inch. Section this illustration as a full section or half section.

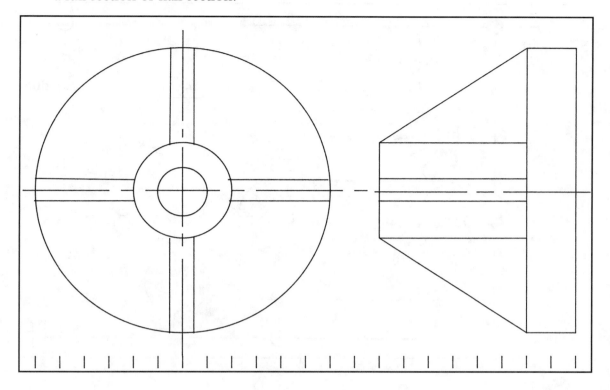

13. Recreate the drawing shown. Copy the contour lines as closely as possible. Include the missing angles on your drawing. Pick a typical civil scale, such as 1 inch = 30 feet, and figure the distance of each leg of the drawing (for example, figure the distance from 2 to 3). Rotate the drawing so that the 4 to 5 side is on the bottom and becomes the side facing a street. Make the text readable from the bottom.

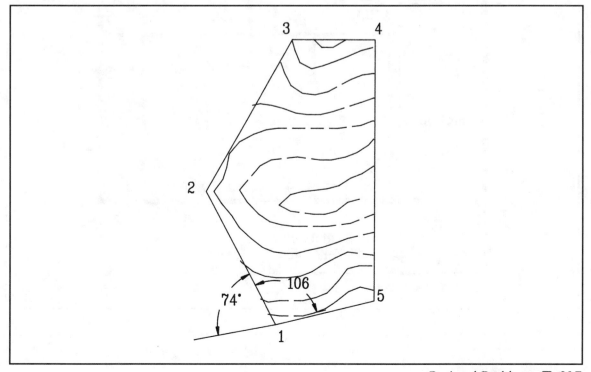

14. Draw the schematic below. You may change the schematic to your liking. For example, change it to fill the screen area or include other electronic symbols.

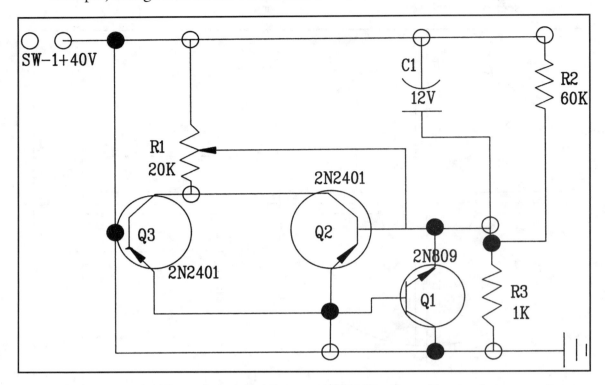

15. Draw the floor plan shown. Set the grid to .25 inch intervals so that the divisions represent .25 inch = 5 feet.

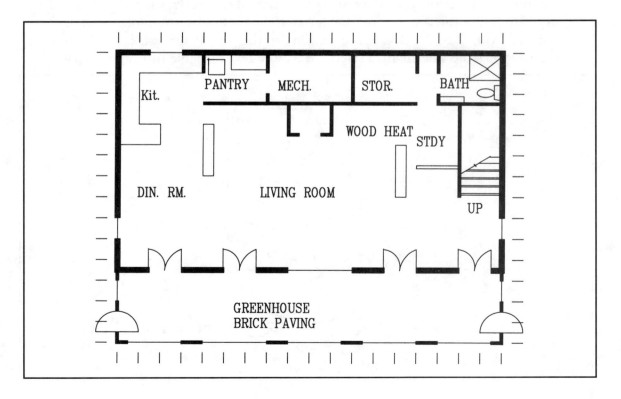

16. Draw a bar graph like the one shown. Use a snap-to-grid setting to help you create the amounts within the graph. Then create your own graph using a hatch or line pattern that you have made.

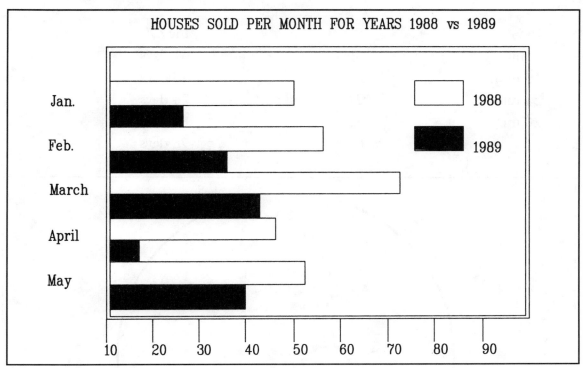

17. Create a large circle like the one in the drawing below. Then create pie charts using the following divisions.

Pie A	Pie B	Pie C
4 min.	36%	61 days
15 min.	23%	43 days
21 min.	21%	74 days
20 min.	12%	89 days
	8	98 days

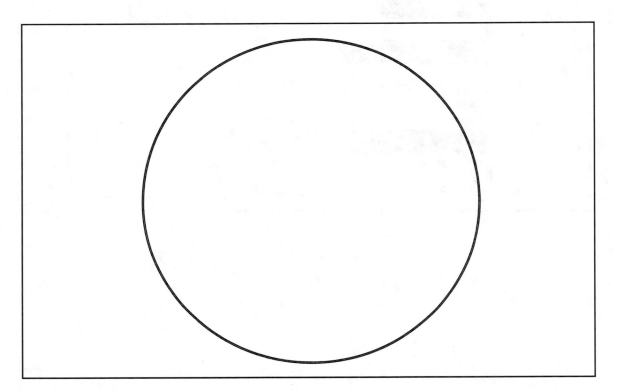

18. Draw the pattern shown below. Make each block 2 inches square, with 1/4 inch folding tabs. Plot the drawing. Then cut out, fold, and tape the pattern.

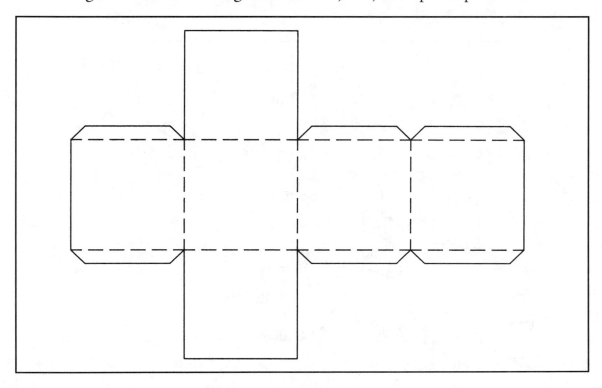

19. Use the sample drawing ENGINE and commands you have learned to copy the following drawing. (For example, use Copy, Mirror, Line, Text, Erase, Fill, and so on.)

20. Draw the figure below to the sizes shown. Create center lines using polar coordinates. Use the Fillet command at .5 inch radius, the Break command, and a snap-to-grid at .5 inch.

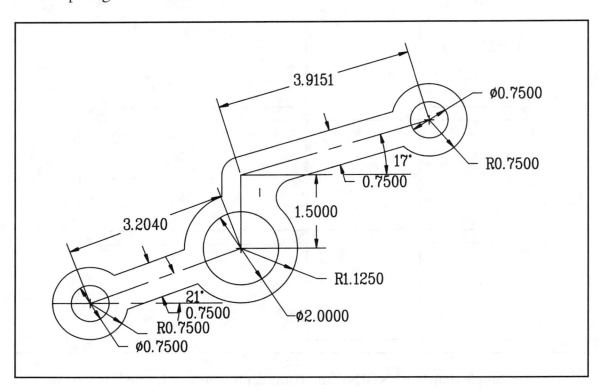

Importing AutoSketch® Drawings into WordPerfect® Text Files

In this activity, you will learn how to copy AutoSketch drawings to a file (document) in a word processing program. Word processors are powerful programs for creating text. When you import a drawing, you can create a document that has both text and drawings. For example, you might write a story and illustrate it with a drawing you created in AutoSketch. This way, you can take advantage of both the drawing power of AutoSketch and the word processing power of a program like WordPerfect.

The word processing program you need for this activity is WordPerfect 5.1.

Opening a WordPerfect File

1. Create and save a file in Wordperfect.

This is the file that the drawing will be transferred to. You might want to name it SKETCH.

2. Exit from Wordperfect.

Preparing the Drawing

1. Load AutoSketch and create a drawing.

To import an AutoSketch drawing into a WordPerfect file, you must first convert it to a DXF file.

2. Select the **Files** menu and the **Make DXF** command.

A dialogue box appears on the screen where you will name the DXF file to be created.

3. Type in a name.

The name you type in depends upon where the WordPerfect file you want to transfer to is located. For example, if the WordPerfect file named SKETCH is in the C drive in a directory called WP51, you would type the following:

    C:\WP51\SKETCH

4. Close the dialogue box.

AutoSketch creates a DXF file and places it in the drive and directory that you have typed. The new file has a DXF extension. For example, if you named the file SKETCH the new name is SKETCH.DXF.

5. Exit from AutoSketch.

Converting the DXF File to a WordPerfect WPG File

1. At the DOS prompt, change to the subdirectory where you have WordPerfect stored.

2. At the DOS prompt, type **GRAPHCNV** and press **Enter**.

3. Type in the name of the DXF file you wish to convert to WordPerfect. If you followed the example above, type in the following:

    C:\WP51\SKETCH.DXF

Don't forget to type in the DXF extension.

4.   Enter the name of the WordPerfect output file.

A new name will appear by default. If you wish to create a different name, type it in.
Be sure to use the extension WPG. For example:

  C:\WP51\SKETCH.WPG

5.   Press **Enter**.

WordPerfect now copies the DXF file and converts it to a WPG file. The original DXF
file is no longer necessary.

Loading the WPG File into a Document

1.   Load WordPerfect.

2.   Use a new file or retrieve a file created earlier (such as the document you opened
     when you first began this activity).

3.   Select **GRAPHICS (Alt-F9).**

4.   Enter **1** to select the Figure option.

5.   Enter **1** to select the Create option.

6.   Enter **1** to select the Filename option.

7.   Enter the name of the file (created earlier) with the WPG extension. Include the
     drive and directory where it is stored.

8.   Press **F7** to go back to the word processing file.

You will see a figure box that shows where the drawing will go.

9.   To see the drawing, press **Print (Shift-F7)** and **Show Document (6).**

10. Press **F7** to go back to the document.

11. Type in some new text. Use Print and Show Document to see what happens.

12. When you are finished creating the document, try printing it.

13. Exit from WordPerfect.

Using DOS

DOS (disk operating system) is a type of software used to make a computer function. DOS works with the CPU (electronic "brain") to send information to and receive information from other parts of the computer. For example, this information can turn disk drives on and off or allow outputs to be viewed on a monitor. The operating system allows a software package like AutoSketch to work with the hardware, or electronics, of the computer.

File Names and Extensions

When you store an AutoSketch drawing you create a file with a name that can be up to eight spaces long. In DOS, the file name you have chosen is automatically followed by a period and three additional characters. These three characters are called a file extension.

All files used in the operation of a software program have a file name and extension. A file name usually describes the contents of the file, and the extension gives its function. For example, AutoSketch drawing files have the extension SKD. By looking at the file extension, you can tell that the file is a drawing.

Some other common file extensions are EXE, COM, DFX, and SHP. File names and extensions can be changed. Some must stay as they are, though, because the operating system (DOS) looks for certain types of files in order to do its job. For example, in order for AutoSketch to work, DOS looks for a file called SKETCH.EXE. The extension EXE comes from the word "execute," which means "to carry out."

Directories and Subdirectories

The drawing files you create build up in the same location as the files that make up the AutoSketch software. After some time, the size of your files will get bigger, and you will have more of them. The storage devices in your computer are like a file cabinet that becomes stuffed full. Your computer begins to operate slower and slower as it searches through these files.

The solution to this problem is to put files into directories and subdirectories. Directories divide the root directory (disk or hard disk) into smaller systems. Subdirectories do the same thing, except that they are smaller systems within the directory. The computer needs to only look for files in the directory or subdirectory, instead of searching every file on the computer system.

You can change to a directory or subdirectory by using the DOS command CD (Change Directory). To create a directory, use the MD (Make Directory) command. The RD (Remove Directory) command removes a directory from the system.

▶ *Hint:*

For more information on DOS or DOS commands, refer to the DOS manual that came with your computer.

DOS Commands Most Often Used With AutoSketch

CD   **Change Directory.** Used to change the current directory.

At the DOS prompt, type **CD** and the name of the new directory or subdirectory. Then press **Enter**. To get back to the root directory, type **CD** and press **Enter**.

CHKDSK   **Check Disk.** Used to check for bad sectors or a damaged disk.

At the DOS prompt, enter the **CHKDSK** command. For example, type **CHKDSK C:** and press **Enter**.

The program checks the disk and tells you the total bytes of disk space, file information, bytes available on disk, bytes of total memory, and bytes free to be used.

CLS   **Clear Screen.** Clears the screen of everything except the DOS prompt.

Type **CLS** at the DOS prompt and press **Enter**.

COPY

Copy. Permits you to copy files from one disk to another.

At the DOS prompt, enter the **COPY** Command, the name of the file, and the disk drive you want to copy to.
Here's an example of how to copy one file from a hard disk drive to a disk. At the C prompt, type **COPY filename.ext A:** and press **Enter**. (Substitute the name and extension of the file you want to copy).

To copy all the files to a disk, type **COPY *.* A:** and press **Enter**.

DATE

Date. Displays the current date.

Type **DATE:** and press **Enter**.

This command displays the current date if it was first entered when the system was turned on. If your computer has a built-in calendar, the date will be displayed even if you did not enter it.

DEL

Delete. Used to erase a file.

At the DOS prompt, enter the **DEL** command. For example, at the C prompt, type **DEL filename.ext** and press **Enter**. (Substitute the name and extension of the file you want to delete).

DIR

Directory. Allows you to view the contents of the current directory or disk, along with the size of each file and the date the file was created.

At the prompt, type **DIR** and press **Enter**.

You can view the directory a couple of other ways, such as **DIR/W** AND **DIR/P**. The *W* means the directory will come up the wide way across the screen, and the *P* means that the directory pauses after the screen is filled.

DISKCOPY

Diskcopy. Copies the entire contents of one disk onto another disk.

Insert the source disk into drive A. Insert a blank disk into drive B. At the A prompt type **DISKCOPY A:B:**.

MD

Make Directory. Creates a new directory or subdirectory.

To create a directory, type **MD**, the name of directory, and press **Enter**. To create a subdirectory, type **MD**, the name of the directory, \, and the name of the subdirectory. For example, type **MD SKETCH\DRAWING**.

MORE <

Displays the contents of the file on the screen, one screen at a time.

Type **MORE** < and the name of the file. For example, type **MORE < filename.ext.**

PRINT   Prints the contents of the file.

Type **PRINT** and the name of the file. For example, type **PRINT filename.ext.**

REN   **Rename.** Used to rename a file.

You must enter the old and the new file names. You also need to select the disk location, if not on the same disk. For example, type **REN C: old filename.ext C: new file name.ext** and press **Enter**. (Substitute the names and extensions of the file you want to rename.)

RD   **Remove Directory.** Used to remove (erase) a directory or subdirectory.

Before you can use this command, you must remove the files from the directory or subdirectory. See the DEL command in this appendix for how to remove files.

After the files are deleted, type **RD** and the name of the directory. Then press **Enter**. For example, press **RD SKETCH**.

TIME   **Time.** Displays the current time.

Type **TIME** and press **Enter**.

This command displays the current time if the time was entered when the system was turned on. If your computer has a built-in clock, the date will be displayed even if you did not enter it.

TYPE   **Type.** Displays the contents of a file on the screen.

At the DOS prompt, enter the **TYPE** command. For example, type **TYPE A:filename.ext** and press **Enter**. (Substitute the name of the disk drive and the file you want to display).

VER   **Version.** Displays the current version (number) of DOS on the screen. Type **VER** and press **Enter**.

Using Disks and Disk Drives

When you format a disk, or use one to save and retrieve AutoSketch files, the computer tells you to insert a disk into a disk drive. Before you can do this, you need to know what kind you have and how to insert the disk into the disk drive.

5 1/4-Inch Disks

If you have a disk that measures 5 1/4 inches square, it could be one of two types: 360 kilobyte or 1.2 megabyte. These disks look very much the same. The main difference between them is that a 1.2 megabyte disk holds a greater amount of information.

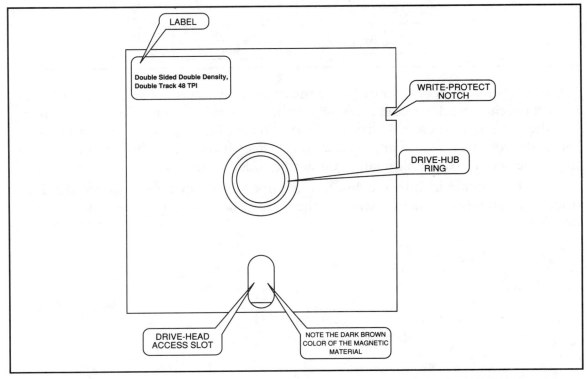

How can you tell which type of disk you have? First, check the label. Does it have abbreviations or wording such as DS (Double Sided) and DD (Double Density)? If so, it is a 360 kilobyte disk. It might also say SS (Soft Sector) or Single Track. If the disk has no label, you can still identify it by looking for the following features: a dark brown color on the disk itself and a drive-hub ring layered on one side.

If your disk does not fit the description above, does it have a label with abbreviations or wording like DS (Double Sided), HD (High Density), and DT 96 TPI (Double Track 96 capacity)? If so, it is a 1.2 megabyte disk. If the disk has no label, look for these features: a black or dark gray color on the disk and the absence of a drive-hub ring on either side.

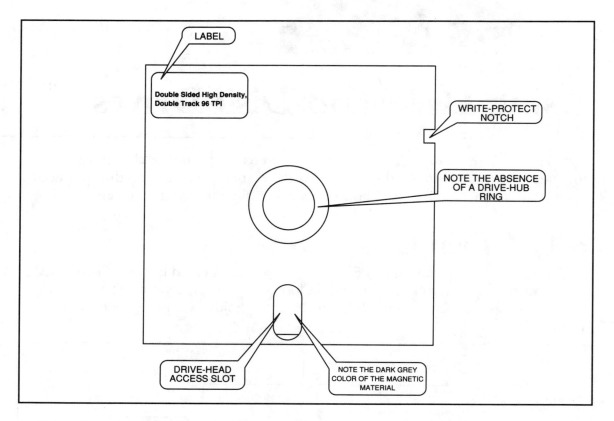

Other features to note on the disk are the drive-head access slot and the write-protect notch. The drive-head access slot is the rectangular opening in the disk cover that the computer uses to read from and write to the disk. The write-protect notch allows the computer to add information to the disk. If you cover the notch with a tab that came with the disk, information cannot be added by mistake.

Now that you can identify the disk and its parts, which way does it go into the disk drive? The answer depends on whether the receiver slot is in the horizontal or vertical position.

If your drive is horizontal, grasp the disk so that the drive-head access slot is facing the computer and the write-protect notch is to the left. The drawing below shows where the drive-head access slot and the write-protect notch are located with respect to each other.

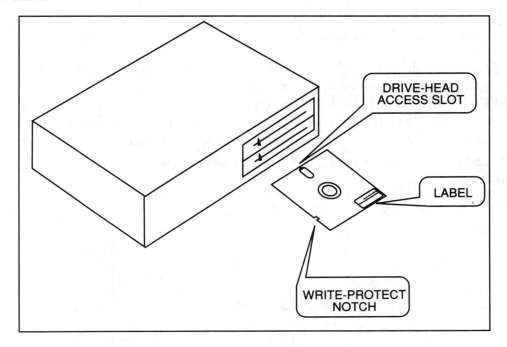

If your disk drive is vertical, grasp the disk so that the drive-head access slot is facing the computer and the write-protect notch faces downward. Once you have positioned it correctly, insert the disk into the receiver slot of the disk drive. Then, push the disk forward as far as possible, without bending the side, and close the latch door. You are now ready to format a disk or save and retrieve drawings.

Like disks, your disk drive may be one of two types: 360 kilobyte or 1.2 megabyte. The disk used must be compatible with the disk drive. Can you use a 360 kilobyte disk in a 1.2 megabyte disk drive? The answer is yes, if you wish to only retrieve files from that disk. If you wish to save files on it, the answer is no. Can you use a 1.2 megabyte disk in a 360 kilobyte disk drive? The answer is no. This disk is incompatible for both retrieving or saving in a 360 kilobyte disk drive.

3 1/2-Inch Disks

A disk that measures 3 1/2 inches square could be either a 720 kilobyte disk or a 1.44 megabyte disk. These types of disks are usually labeled DD for double density (720 Kilobyte) or HD for high density (1.44 megabyte). Double density disks are also referred to as low density disks.

You must use a 3 1/2-inch disk in a 3 1/2-inch disk drive. In other words, don't try to use one in a 5 1/2-inch drive. You should also use a disk and disk drive that are compatible. For example, use a low density (720 kilobyte) disk with a low density drive.

▶ *Note:*

A 1.44 megabyte drive can be set to format low density disks by adding certain parameters when you use the Format command. For example, you might type FORMAT/4. See your DOS manual.

The disks have a drive-head access slot used to read and write to the disk. The slot is covered by a metal plate that is also the disk's label. On the under side of the disks you will find a write-protect switch. If the switch is up, the computer can read and write information to the disk. If the switch is down, the computer can only read from the disks. That way, wrong information cannot be added by mistake.

These disks have an arrow on the label side. Insert a disk with the arrow pointing towards the disk drive.

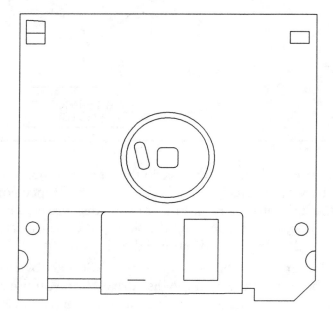

▶ *Hint:*

Disk drives are labeled, or referred to, as A, B, C, or D. If you have one disk drive, it is designated A, and two disk drives are designated A and B. One hard disk is usually labeled C, and two hard disks are labeled C and D. The drive label designation is decided upon when the computer system is configured.

Formatting a Disk

Formatting is the process of creating tracks on a new disk. These tracks are necessary in order for your computer and software to save and retrieve files. Without formatting, your software is unable to save your AutoSketch drawings on a disk.

Your computer accepts only formatted disks from IBM or compatible computers, so don't use disks formatted by other types. The formatting procedure varies, depending upon the type of equipment you have and where the DOS (Disk Operating System) for each type is stored.

Machines equipped with one or two disk drives and a hard disk drive will normally store the DOS Operations files on the hard disk drive. They are also usually stored in a subdirectory, and you must change to the subdirectory before you can format a disk.

Here are the steps to follow:

1.   Type CD/ and the name of the subdirectory where DOS is located.

See Appendix A for an explanation of the DOS command CD. If you need to find the subdirectory where DOS is located, use the DOS command DIR to get a list of subdirectories and files.

2.   Type **FORMAT A:** or **FORMAT B:**.

Use the drive label of the disk drive you will use to format a new disk.

▶ *Warning:*

Never use the drive labels C or D unless you intend to format your hard disk drive. If you do, the drive will be formatted, and you will permanently remove all files stored on it.

After step 2, the computer reads the Format file and places it in memory. The monitor then displays a message like this: "Insert new disk for drive A: and strike ENTER when ready."

3.   Insert a new disk in drive A or B.

4.   Press the **ENTER** key.

After Formatting the Disk

After you have formatted a disk, your monitor will display the following information:

- total bytes of storage in disk
- number of bad sectors on the disk (if any)
- number of bytes available in your disk

The computer then asks you if you want to format another disk.

1.   If you want to format another disk, insert a new one and press **Y**.
2.   Press **Enter** and follow the computer's instructions.
3.   If you do not want to format another disk, press **N** and **Enter**.

The formatted disk is now ready for saving and retrieving files.

▶ *Hint:*

If you encounter bad sectors in this segment of the formatting routine, format the same disk again. If you still see bad sectors, don't use the disk. The best thing to do is discard the disk or return it to the place where you bought it.

Command Glossary

ALIGN DIMENSION	Places a measurement between two selected points, including the value for the distance and arrowheads at the ends of the line.
ANGLE	Used to measure the distance between two points that give direction, or bearing, from a base point.
ANGLE DIMENSION	Used to add dimensions to angles.
ARC	A part of a circle made by entering three points: a starting point, a point on the arc, and an endpoint.
ARC MODE	Changes the way the Polyline command works. When ARC MODE is on, the Polyline command draws a series of connected arcs.
AREA	Used to measure the inside and distance around a drawing.
ARROW	Used to change the style of arrowhead used when dimensioning.
ATTACH	Used in the Assist menu when you want to draw new objects that should adhere exactly to a particular part on a drawing. Used in the Settings menu to turn on and off the types of Attach points listed in the dialogue box.
BEARING	Used to measure the direction in degrees from your last location.
BOX	Used to draw a rectangular object with a starting point and a second point. You determine the size of the box as you drag towards the second point.

BOX ARRAY   Used in the Change menu to create rows and columns of figures that are exact copies of one original. Used in the Settings menu to set up the box array.

BREAK   Uses break points to remove one end or any part of a line or object.

CHAMFER   Used in the Change menu to place a beveled edge on the corner of an object. Used in the Settings menu to set up the size and angle of the chamfer.

CIRCLE   Used to create a complete circle by selecting the center point and dragging the outside edge to any size.

COLOR   A method of selecting the color used for drawing an object on the screen.

COORDINATES   Displays the coordinates of the pointer. The coordinates change as the pointer moves.

COPY   Used to make a duplicate of any screen object and move it to another position, without changing the original.

CURVE   Used in the Draw menu to create a smooth, curved line that goes through the first and last point selected and is pulled toward all other points. Used in the Settings menu to decide how exactly AutoSketch draws segments of a curve.

DISTANCE   Used to determine the exact measurement between any two points on a drawing.

ELLIPSE   Used on the Draw menu for creating an ellipse. On the Settings menu, this command provides three methods for creating an ellipse.

ERASE   Removes drawing elements from the screen.

FILL   Works with the Polyline and Pattern Fill commands on the Draw menu. For example, if Fill is turned off, the pattern does not appear.

FILLET   Used in the Change menu to place a smooth arc on the corner of an object. Used in the Settings menu to set up the radius of the fillet.

FRAME   Used to turn the frame on and off when using the Curve command.

GAME   Allows you to play a game included with the AutoSketch program.

GRID   Used in the Assist menu to display dots in a rectangular pattern as set up with the Settings menu.

GROUP   Allows you to gather up to 100 objects and select them all by picking one point.

HORIZONTAL DIMENSION	Used to insert a horizontal dimension between two points.
INFORMATION	Shows the current AutoSketch version and serial number.
LAST PLOT BOX	Fills the screen with the last plot box created.
LAST VIEW	Allows you to quickly move between the current view and the last view displayed.
LAYER	Used to select the current layer and choose which layers are shown on the screen.
LIMITS	Used to select the drawing size from the bottom left to the upper right corner.
LINE	Used to create a line by selecting a starting point, dragging to a desired distance, and an end point.
LINE TYPE	Used to select a different type of line to draw new objects on the current layer.
MAKE DXF	Turns the current drawing into a Drawing Interchange Format file so it can be used in other software programs.
MAKE SLIDE	Produces an AutoCAD slide of your drawing so it can be used later in other AutoCAD drawings and presentations.
MIRROR	Draws a mirror image of an object, without changing the original.
MOVE	Used to move one or more objects anywhere on the drawing area by selecting a base point and an insertion point.
NEW	Used to clear the current drawing from the screen and start a new one.
OPEN	Used to select an existing drawing that has been saved.
ORTHO	Used when you want to draw only vertically and horizontally.
PAN	Used to move the whole drawing without changing its size or substance.
PART	Used to create a library of drawings that can be inserted into other drawings as many times as desired.
PART BASE	Used to mark a point for an insertion base.
PART CLIP	Takes from a drawing segments to be added to another drawing.
PATTERN	Provides patterns to choose from.
PATTERN FILL	Used to draw filled objects.
PEN INFO	Used to set up a pen plotter.

PEN INFO	Used to set up a pen plotter.
PICK	Used to adjust the value of the the pick interval.
PLAY MACRO	Used to run a macro.
PLOT	The hard copy (paper) output of a screen drawing.
PLOT AREA	Used to select plotting elements for a drawing before it is sent to the plotter.
PLOT NAME	Used to choose the name of the drawing for the output file.
POINT	Used in the Draw menu to draw a dot or reference point at a precise location on the screen. Used in the Measure menu to display coordinates of the pointer as you move it around the screen area.
POLYLINE	A linked arrangement of lines that can be closed to form a polygon.
PRINT	PRINT, PRINT AREA, PRINT NAME -- Commands that appear instead of corresponding PLOT commands when AutoSketch is configured for a printer.
PROPERTY	Used in the Change menu to carry out the changes in color, layer, and line type selected in the Settings menu.
QUICK TEXT	Used on the Draw menu for adding lettering, dimensions, and notes to drawings.
QUIT	Used to quit the AutoSketch program.
READ DXF	Inputs files from AutoCAD and other software programs that have output files in a DXF format.
RECORD MACRO	Used to record a series of actions that you want AutoSketch to perform by itself.
REDO	Used to move through all the prior Undo selections.
REDRAW	Used to clean up a drawing after editing objects.
RING ARRAY	Used in the Change menu to place exact copies of one object in a circular pattern set up with the Settings menu.
ROTATE	Used to rotate the position of an object around a base point within a full circle.
SAVE	Used to record a drawing on disk.
SAVE AS	Used to give the drawing on the screen a new name.
SCALE	Used to enlarge or reduce an object by dragging from a base point to the desired size.
SHOW PROPERTIES	Used as a reference to reveal the color, layer, and line type of an item in a drawing.

SNAP	Used in the Assist menu to automatically pick a point. Used in the Settings menu to turn on or off the Snap mode and to pick the snap spacing.
STRETCH	Used to alter an object by attaching to the stretch base and extending it to a new length or form.
TEXT	Used in the Settings menu to control the text characteristics.
TEXT EDITOR	Provides a dialogue box for adding and changing text. When used on the Draw menu, text can be changed within the dialogue box before adding it to the screen. When used on the Change menu, existing text can be changed.
UNDO	Used to go backwards through the sequence used in creating a drawing.
UNGROUP	Breaks up a grouped set of objects into single objects.
UNITS	Sets up the type of unit (decimal or architectural) displayed while using AutoSketch.
USER INPUT	Used when creating macros.
VERTICAL DIMENSION	Used to insert a vertical measurement between two points.
VIEW ICONS	Used to determine whether drawings, fonts, and patterns are listed by icons or by names.
VIEW SLIDE	Used to look at a slide file from either AutoSketch or AutoCAD.
ZOOM BOX	Changes the view of a drawing, usually to enlarge a particular part within a window. The window is defined by choosing two points.
ZOOM FULL	Used to expand the drawing to display only the section having objects within.
ZOOM LIMITS	Used to redraw the screen area in units that you define for the lower left corner and upper right corner.
ZOOM X	A fast method of enlarging or reducing a drawing on the screen, while keeping it centered.

A

B

C